Within Limits

The U.S. Air Force and the Korean War

Wayne Thompson
and Bernard C. Nalty

Air Force History and Museums Program
1996

Within Limits

The U.S. Air Force and the Korean War

Despite American success in preventing the conquest of South Korea by communist North Korea, the Korean War of 1950–1953 did not satisfy Americans who expected the kind of total victory they had experienced in World War II. In that earlier, larger war, victory over Japan came after two atomic bombs destroyed the cities of Hiroshima and Nagasaki. But in Korea five years later, the United States limited itself to conventional weapons. Even after communist China entered the war, Americans put China off-limits to conventional bombing as well as nuclear bombing. Operating within these limits, the U.S. Air Force helped to repel two invasions of South Korea while securing control of the skies so decisively that other United Nations forces could fight without fear of air attack.

Invasion

Before dawn on Sunday, June 25, 1950, communist North Korea attacked South Korea, storming across the improvised border that divided the peninsula into two countries. Some five years earlier, when Japan surrendered, the United States had proposed that American forces disarm Japanese forces in Korea south of the 38th parallel and Soviet troops perform the same task north of that line. Once the Japanese had been disarmed and repatriated, Korea was at last to become independent after almost fifty years of domination by Japan. This scenario depended on continued cooperation between the Soviet Union and the United States, but the wartime alliance soon collapsed. Instead of a unified nation, two rival states came to share the Korean peninsula. The Soviet Union supported the Democratic People's Republic of Korea, or North Korea, under the leadership of Kim Il Sung, a shadowy figure who had fought the Japanese and fled to the Soviet Union where he apparently served in the armed forces. The United States stood behind the Republic of Korea, or South Korea, headed by seventy-year-old Syngman Rhee, an implacable foe of the Japanese who had earned a doctorate at Princeton University before World War I, returned to his homeland only to be expelled in 1921 by the Japanese, and spent the next twenty-five years in exile campaigning for Korean independence. When the newly constituted national assembly elected Rhee president of South Korea in August 1948, the United States terminated the military government that had ruled the South and began withdrawing its occupation forces.

Syngman Rhee and Kim Il Sung, headed opposing governments on an arbitrarily divided peninsula. The 38th parallel did not conform to any natural feature that might have separated North from South. In fact, the two Koreas complemented each other; in the North were the industries developed by the Japanese, while in the South, where two-thirds of the people lived, the principal activity was farming. Given the interdependence of the two regions and the ambitions of their leaders, some sort of clash was inevitable. Soon insurgents directed from the North were challenging the authority of President Rhee, who responded by trying to suppress all dissent in the South, whether communist-inspired or not.

To maintain the independence of South Korea, American military advisers trained and equipped a lightly armed force, basically a constabulary, believed capable of maintaining order and if necessary resisting an invasion, although too weak to embark on the liberation of North Korea. Confidence in the defensive ability of the South Korean armed services later seemed hard to justify, for the nation had only 100,000 soldiers, who lacked tanks and heavy artillery; a small coast guard; and an air force that consisted of fewer than 20 liaison aircraft or trainers, with just 36 of 57 pilots fully qualified to fly them. In contrast, North Korea had an army of at least 130,000 combat troops, who were supported by some 500 tanks and artillery pieces ranging in size to 122 millimeters. The North Korean air arm possessed 132 combat airplanes supplied by the Soviet Union, all first-line types during World War II, including the Ilyushin Il–10 attack aircraft and the Yakovlev Yak–3 and Yak–7 fighters.

Although North Korea depended on the Soviet Union and South Korea needed the assistance of the United States, both Kim Il Sung and Syngman Rhee were capable of independent action. Rhee's popularity stemmed in part from his denunciation of an American plan, revealed in December 1945, for the creation of a provisional government under a five-year international trusteeship as a step toward self-government. Rhee succeeded in marshaling demonstrations against what he considered a new form of colonialism, and the scheme collapsed, undermined as much by increasing hostility between the United States and the Soviet Union as by the opposition of the South Korean leader. Similarly, Kim could ignore the fact that his Soviet sponsors considered him a counterweight to the influence of Chinese communism and turn to China when the Soviet Union seemed lukewarm to his ambitions for unifying Korea.

As the decade of the 1940s drew to a close, Korea seemed less important than several potentially dangerous areas that competed for the attention of the American government. In the aftermath of the Berlin blockade, the Truman administration had concentrated on Europe, even though its basic national policy called for opposing the spread of communism anywhere in the world. The United States had already begun to invest heavily in the economic recovery of western Europe and encouraging a

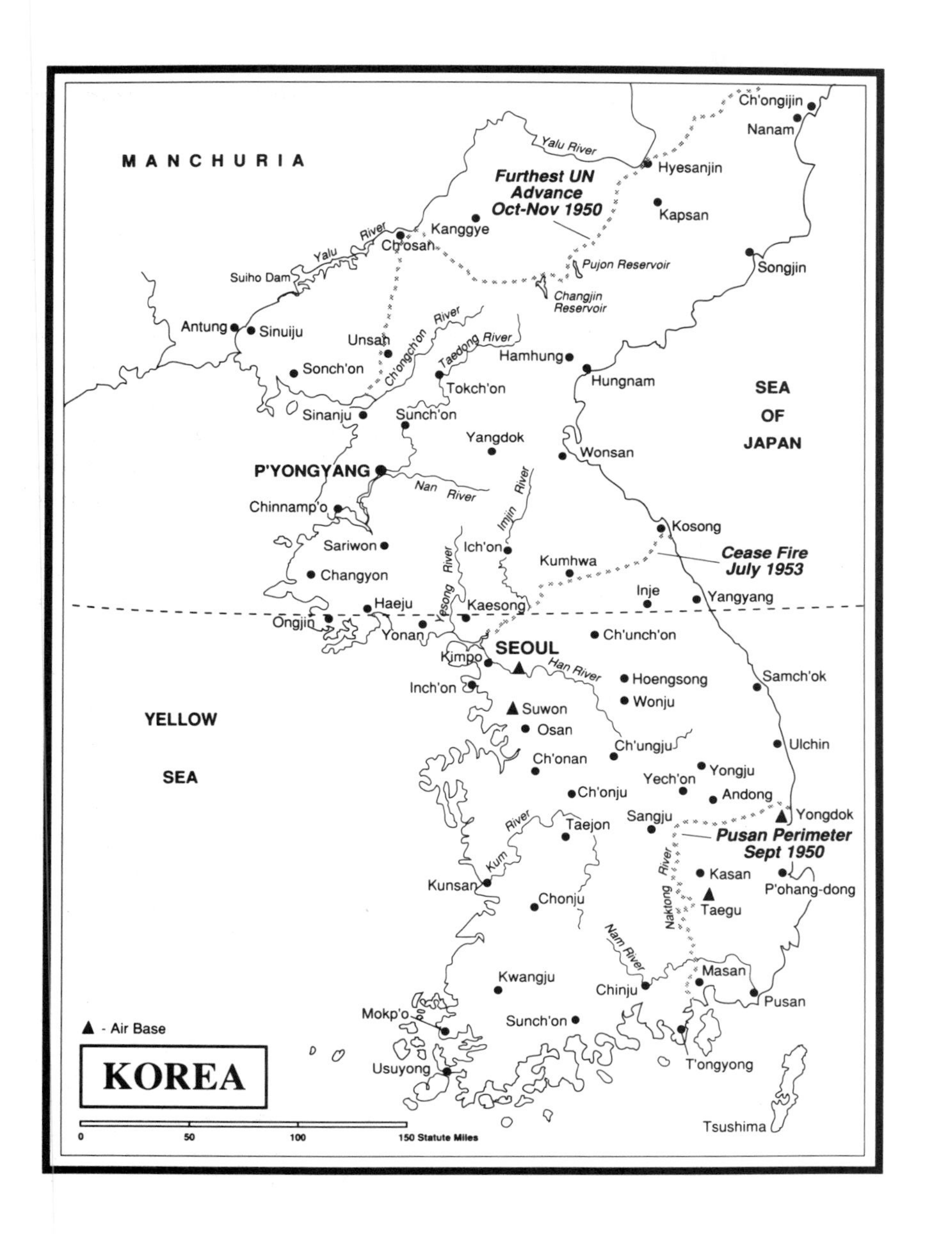
MANCHURIA
Furthest UN Advance Oct-Nov 1950
Yalu River
Ch'ongijin
Nanam
Hyesanjin
Kapsan
Kanggye
Ch'osan
Pujon Reservoir
Changjin Reservoir
Songjin
Suiho Dam
Antung
Sinuiju
Unsan
Ch'ongch'on River
Taedong River
Hamhung
Sonch'on
Tokch'on
Hungnam
SEA OF JAPAN
Sinanju
Sunch'on
Yangdok
Wonsan
P'YONGYANG
Nan River
Imjin River
Chinnamp'o
Kosong
Sariwon
Ich'on
Cease Fire July 1953
Kumhwa
Changyon
Yesong River
Inje
Yangyang
Haeju
Kaesong
Ongjin
Yonan
Ch'unch'on
SEOUL
Kimpo
Han River
Hoengsong
Samch'ok
Inch'on
Wonju
YELLOW SEA
Suwon
Osan
Ch'ungju
Ulchin
Ch'onan
Yongju
Yech'on
Ch'onju
Andong
Sangju
Yongdok
Taejon
Pusan Perimeter Sept 1950
Kum River
Naktong River
Kasan
P'ohang-dong
Kunsan
Taegu
Chonju
Nam River
Masan
Kwangju
Chinju
Pusan
▲ - Air Base
Mokp'o
Sunch'on
KOREA
Usuyong
T'ongyong
Tsushima
0
50
100
150 Statute Miles

military alliance against possible Soviet aggression there. Accomplishing these goals in Europe while strengthening the American position in the Far East at the same time seemed impossible, for the President was determined to prevent the budget deficits that he believed would produce inflation and economic dislocation. In Asia, therefore, the wisest course seemed to be to avoid specific commitments, except to the defense of Japan, in hope of creating uncertainty among the Chinese and Soviet leaders as to how the United States might react in a crisis. Unfortunately, American ambiguity did not cause hesitation, but instead gave the clear impression of indifference to the fate of South Korea.

Often singled out as being especially unfortunate in its probable interpretation by North Korea and its allies is a speech by Secretary of State Dean G. Acheson in which he declared that the Philippines, the Ryukyus, Japan, and the Aleutians formed the limit of the American defensive arc in the western Pacific. Whether trying to create uncertainty among the communist leaders or to emphasize America's belief in the possibility of a peaceful settlement of the friction between the two Koreas, he may well have given the impression that South Korea would not be defended. Such a conclusion, however, might also have been drawn from the withdrawal of American occupation troops and, afterward, from congressional indifference to economic aid for South Korea.

Because of the strategic importance of Japan, the United States maintained there a seemingly large occupation force, consisting of four of the Army's ten divisions, but all four were understrength, only partially equipped with tanks and artillery, and poorly prepared for combat. These divisions formed the Eighth Army, under Lt. Gen. Walton H. Walker, who was directly responsible to the Commander in Chief, Far East Command, General of the Army Douglas MacArthur, who also served as Supreme Commander, Allied Powers, in the continuing occupation of Japan. When North Korea attacked the South, MacArthur's Far East Command was responsible for the defense of Japan, the Philippines, and the Ryukyus. Since the withdrawal of the occupation troops from South Korea, the general was concerned only with the administrative and logistic support of the Korean Military Advisory Group and the American embassy at the capital city of Seoul. To assist with the mission of the Far East Command, the Navy provided the Naval Forces, Far East, under Vice Adm. C. Turner Joy. The equivalent Air Force organization was the Far East Air Forces, commanded by Lt. Gen. George E. Stratemeyer.

Described as resembling a genial college professor, General Stratemeyer bore responsibility for maintaining a mobile striking force in support of Army and Navy operations throughout MacArthur's Far East Command. To accomplish this, he had available more than 400 combat aircraft assigned to air bases in Japan, Okinawa, and Guam, and the Philippines. As was true of the ground forces, the largest concentration of aerial strength was in Japan, where the Fifth Air Force, under Maj. Gen. Earle E. "Pat" Partridge, was flying eight squadrons of F–80s, two of B–26 light bombers (known as A–26s during World War II), and three of F–82 Twin Mustang all-weather interceptors. One squadron of F–51s from the Royal Australian Air Force shared Iwakuni airfield on the island of Honshu with Partridge's B–26s, but the Australians reported directly to MacArthur as Supreme Commander, Allied Powers, and merely maintained liaison with Stratemeyer's headquarters. Assigned to the Far East Air Forces and located in Japan were a variety of rescue aircraft and three squadrons of transports. A group of B–29s, equipped solely for conventional bombing, was based on Guam and belonged to the Twentieth Air Force, also a part of Stratemeyer's Far East Air Forces.

Although the Fifth Air Force gave the impression of aerial might located near the scene of the fighting in South Korea, this was largely an illusion. Most of its aircraft were F–80 jet fighters, which did not have the range to intervene effectively from their normal bases in Japan; and Partridge's airmen had little practice supporting troops in combat. This deficiency resulted from the recent emphasis within the Air Force on strategic bombing; the merger of the tactical and air defense missions in the Continental Air Command, which greatly complicated training in the United States; and the lack of space for large-scale exercises involving air and ground units on Japan's densely populated islands.

In Korea the kind of local attack anticipated by the framers of NSC–68 had indeed occurred. Clearly the policy of the Truman administration to resist the further expansion of communism demanded intervention, regardless of the region and the possible impact on the defense budget and the nation's economy. Yet, even as the President and his advisers drew a parallel between communist aggression in the Far East and the Nazi conquest of Czechoslovakia (where the western democracies had failed to take a stand that might have prevented World War II), the administration realized that other wars might erupt, possibly in western Europe, considered the principal object of Soviet ambitions. Aggression in Asia had to be stopped, though not at the risk of losing Europe to communism.

When news of the North Korean offensive reached Washington on the evening of June 24, Secretary of State Acheson informed the President, who was visiting his hometown, Independence, Missouri. Mr. Truman agreed to invoke the principle of collective security and try to internationalize the response to the North Korean attack by appealing to the United Nations, then meeting in a temporary headquarters at Lake Success, New York. Because the Soviet delegate to the United Nations Security Council had walked out in protest of the refusal to accept a representative from communist China, he could not exercise his nation's right of veto, and in his absence the United Nations called on North Korea to withdraw beyond the 38th parallel. When that resolution was ignored, with the Soviet delegate still absent, the Security Council on June 27 called on the members of the United Nations to provide South Korea with whatever assistance might be required to repel the invasion and restore peace to the peninsula. The resolution formed the basis for a United Nations Command, activated on July 24, headed by MacArthur with the assistance of the staff of the Far East Command. Even as United Nations commander, however, he was responsible ultimately to the President of the United States rather than to the Secretary General of the United Nations or the Security Council.

By the time the Security Council had called for the United Nations to join forces in defense of South Korea, American aircraft already were flying missions over the embattled country. After returning from Missouri to Washington on June 25, President Truman approved the use of American air and naval forces to help defend South Korea. The Joint Chiefs of Staff set up a teletype conference with MacArthur and relayed to him the President's decision to intervene. While the Chief Executive was reaching this decision, the question of neutralizing Soviet air bases had been addressed. Gen. Hoyt S. Vandenberg, the Air Force Chief of Staff, raised the possibility that atomic bombs might be necessary for this purpose, but Truman saw no need to do more than draft plans for the eventuality.

The authorization to employ air power, even though armed only with conventional weapons and limited to targets in South Korea as the President directed, seemed to have a dramatic effect on General MacArthur, at a time when Seoul, the South Korean capital was about to be abandoned to the advancing enemy. General Partridge found MacArthur to be "almost jubilant" and confident that vigorous action by the Fifth Air Force would drive the North Koreans back in disorder. MacArthur directed Partridge to attack tanks, troop concentrations, and other military targets south of the 38th parallel, while also maintaining the aerial defenses of Japan in the event the Soviet Union should extend the war there.

Partridge promised that light bombers would hit targets in South Korea on Tuesday, June 27, the third day of the North Korean attack, but he could not meet his self-imposed deadline. A half-dozen of the B–26s were providing air cover for a ship pressed into service to evacuate American civilians from the port of Inchon, and bad weather forced those sent against enemy armor to turn back. Not until Wednesday morning, June 28, after 1st Lt. Bryce Poe in an RF–80 had flown the Air Force's first jet combat reconnaissance mission, did twelve B–26s make the first American air strike since the invasion. The bombers hit the railroad yard at Munsan near the 38th parallel and then strafed tracks and highways nearby. Later in the day four B–29s patrolled the four main routes over which the North Koreans were advancing, attacking targets of opportunity.

Despite weather that had forced the B–26s to turn back, on Tuesday, June 27, Air Force transports, escorted by fighters, began flying American civilians out of Kimpo airfield near Seoul. At about noon, five North American F–82s encountered five Yaks over Kimpo and downed three of the Russian-built fighters. A few hours later, eight North Korean Il–10s tried to strafe the airfield, but four F–80s, operating at extreme range to protect the evacuation, destroyed four of the attackers. Some 2,000 Americans were evacuated, half by ship and half by air.

A few minutes before the F–82s had destroyed the first of the Yaks over Kimpo, the commander of the Far East Air Forces, General Stratemeyer, returned to Japan from a visit to Washington. Although the initial victories of the Fifth Air Force in aerial combat over Kimpo encouraged him, he believed that the airfields in North Korea would have to be attacked as quickly as possible. The importance of airfields was confirmed on June 28, when Yaks strafed Suwon airfield, some fifteen miles south of Seoul, and destroyed or damaged a B–26, an F–82, and a C–54. Despite the danger at Suwon, MacArthur was determined to visit the place. It had become the command post for the liaison group that he had sent to Korea to report on the situation; and one member of the group, Air Force Lt. Col. John McGinn, had improvised a tactical air control center to handle American aircraft in the vicinity. En route to Suwon on Thursday, June 29, MacArthur approved Stratemeyer's request for authority to strike airfields north of the 38th parallel. Late that same day, as MacArthur was driving back to Suwon from the Han River where he had seen the flood of South Korean troops and refugees streaming away from Seoul, eighteen B–26s dropped fragmentation bombs on the airfield at Pyongyang, the North Korean capital. The B–26s returned without loss, their crews claiming to have destroyed or damaged twenty-five aircraft on the ground and one in the air. News of MacArthur's decision and the resulting attack had not reached Washington several hours later when Truman approved air strikes north of the 38th parallel. The authorization reached MacArthur on June 30 when he returned from Suwon.

Naval aircraft soon joined in attacking the North. When the war broke out, two aircraft carriers, the American *Valley Forge* and the British *Triumph*, along with their supporting warships, were available in Far Eastern waters. The two carriers and their escorts met at Buckner Bay, Okinawa, and steamed toward Korea as Task Force 77, commanded by Vice Adm. Arthur D. Struble of the U.S. Navy. Admiral Joy, who had discussed possible future operations with Struble, conferred with Generals MacArthur and Stratemeyer and agreed to use carrier aircraft against targets in the vicinity of Pyongyang, far beyond the battleline. Consequently, on July 3, British and American squadrons based on the carriers raided the airfield at Haeju and the airfield and rail facilities at Pyongyang; and on the 4th,

Struble launched a second day of strikes against targets near the North Korean capital. From the west coast of Korea, Task Force 77 steamed by way of Okinawa to the Sea of Japan, where on July 18 its aircraft blasted the oil refinery and storage tanks at Wonsan, North Korea, touching off spectacular fires.

Although these early naval air operations were largely confined to the North, Partridge had the mission of attacking the enemy throughout the Korean peninsula, and Stratemeyer set about providing him the necessary men and aircraft, drawing first on the resources of the Far East Air Forces. While Partridge shifted his F–80s—ome fitted with locally manufactured jettisonable fuel tanks to extend their range–to airfields in Japan nearer Korea, Stratemeyer brought in other F–80s from the Philippines and took steps to acquire F–51 Mustangs. The comparatively slow Mustang with its liquid-cooled piston engine was vulnerable to ground fire during strafing missions, but it could operate from the short, unpaved airstrips in southern South Korea. The Australian government entrusted to Stratemeyer's control squadron of F–51s based in Japan, the first military unit made available by a member of the United Nations other than the United States for the defense of South Korea, and the Far East Air Forces began taking Mustangs from storage for assignment to the South Korean Air Force or to a provisional squadron being formed by the Fifth Air Force in Japan. Generals Stratemeyer and Partridge could not expect immediate help from the United States, for no reserve of combat-ready aircraft and trained crews was immediately available. General Vandenberg was able, however, to send two groups of B–29s not scheduled for incorporation into the Strategic Air Command's atomic strike force as reinforcements for the group that had deployed from Guam to Okinawa to be nearer targets in Korea. Also at hand were some 1,500 F–51s, half in storage and half assigned to the Air National Guard. On July 5, the first American ground unit sent to South Korea, a reinforced battalion of perhaps 500 men, placed itself in the path of an advancing North Korean division 20 times its size. By that time, a total of 145 Mustangs had been retrieved from the Air National Guard and prepared for shipment by sea to Japan where Air Force pilots would undergo transitional training before flying the aircraft in combat.

Strategic Bombers and Tactical Problems

Along with two groups of B–29s, Vandenberg sent to the Far East a veteran of World War II, Maj. Gen. Emmett O'Donnell, who had commanded B–17s during the unsuccessful defense of the Philippines and later led B–29 strikes against Japan. After arriving in Japan, he established the Bomber Command, Far East Air Forces, consisting initially of three groups of B–29s. The mission of bomber command encompassed long-range interdiction and destruction of strategic targets, essentially the work done by a similar organization in World War II, and O'Donnell brought with him an appropriate list of targets. Tactical air operations—air superiority, close air support, and interdiction in the vicinity of the battlefield—were the responsibility of Fifth Air Force under General Partridge.

The situation on the ground was becoming too dangerous to permit the division of labor between O'Donnell's bomber command and Fifth Air Force that Stratemeyer had approved on the basis of Air Force doctrine. In the first ground combat of the war by American soldiers, the reinforced battalion assigned to slow the North Korean advance had been overwhelmed in a matter of hours, and a hard-fought delaying action by an entire regiment might gain no more than seventy-two hours. A race was developing between American troops arriving in greater numbers and the advancing enemy. MacArthur and his staff believed that every available aircraft should be used to slow the North Koreans until a defensive perimeter could be established around the port of Pusan in southernmost South Korea. On occasion the headquarters of the Far East Command insisted that the B–29s attack areas close to the battlelines through which the enemy was advancing. Stratemeyer complied but objected to the use of the big bombers against targets better suited to fighter-bombers. Vandenberg, in the Far East on an inspection, supported his subordinate, according to Stratemeyer, "very explicitly and masterfully" explaining the difference between tactical and strategic air operations. After listening to the Air Force Chief of Staff, MacArthur conceded that it was indeed wasteful to use B–29s against the hard-to-locate targets normally hit by fighter-bombers, but in the present emergency he felt he had to hit the enemy with every available airplane. As a result, his headquarters directed that the B–29s be dispatched in mid-July against bridges, road junctions, and troop concentrations within sixty miles of a critical segment of the front lines.

The argument against using strategic bombers in this basically tactical role was taken up by Maj. Gen. Otto P. Weyland, chosen by Vandenberg to serve as Stratemeyer's vice commander for operations. Weyland had earned a brilliant reputation for providing close air support during World War II, when his XIX Tactical Air Command functioned as a part of Vandenberg's Ninth Air Force during the thrust through France in 1944. Confident that his job was to "run the air war," the new vice commander reached Japan in late July 1950 and immediately began whittling away at the influence of MacArthur's chief of staff, Maj. Gen. Edward M. Almond, in the selection of targets for the B–29s. Like almost everyone else on MacArthur's joint staff, Almond was an Army officer. He had, however, attended the Air Corps Tactical School at Maxwell Field in the 1930s and therefore considered himself an expert in military aviation, and for him military aviation included the B–29s, which he felt free to use as he deemed necessary. Since Almond's principal concern was the ground forces fighting in Korea, he tended to ignore the need to disrupt the flow of North Korean supplies and reinforcements, and he concentrated almost exclusively on the battlefield. Convinced that Stratemeyer's discussions with MacArthur and Almond were going nowhere, Weyland took matters into his own hands. Without telling Stratemeyer, he sent a critique of target selection to MacArthur's deputy for operations. As Weyland expected, the memorandum was passed to Almond, who responded by repeating the argument that he needed the B–29s to meet battlefield emergencies. Weyland countered by pointing out that, even though the Pusan perimeter was taking shape and growing stronger, "emergencies" were becoming almost routine. Perhaps, he suggested, Almond needed an airman to determine how the B–29s could be most effective. The army officer agreed that this sort of help might be useful, but he would not give up his access to the bombers. Instead he compromised, retaining control over one group of B–29s while releasing the other two to attack targets chosen by Far East Air Forces. As the North Koreans rushed supplies southward to sustain the offensive, MacArthur agreed that all three groups should be used for long-range interdiction, and B–29s heavily damaged several railroad yards and bridges during August.

While Weyland was working in Tokyo to shift the focus of B–29 operations away from the battlefield to targets in North Korea, Vandenberg was making preparations in Washington for a strategic bombing campaign against the North that was modeled after similar operations in World War II. He persuaded the Joint Chiefs of Staff to send to the Far East two additional groups of B–29s for attacking industrial targets north of the 38th parallel, increasing Bomber Command to five groups totaling more than 100 Superfortresses. The Joint Chiefs also provided a target list, prepared like the one already given General O'Donnell by intelligence specialists of the Strategic Air Command. The principal targets on the second list were the chemical plants at Hungnam, believed to produce radioactive material (for the Soviet atomic energy program) as well as conventional explosives and fertilizer; the munitions factories at Pyongyang; an oil refinery at Wonsan; and the oil storage facilities at Rashin. Before his B–29s were diverted almost exclusively to targets closer to the battlelines, O'Donnell had bombed the port of Wonsan and a nitrogen plant at Hungnam. Because of their compact size—only the capital of Pyongyang, with a population of 500,000, had more than 100,000 inhabitants—and lack of fireproof buildings, North Korean towns seemed almost as vulnerable to fire bombs as the cities of Japan, which O'Donnell had helped reduce to ashes during World War II. This time, however, the Truman administration would not let him use incendiaries against cities and instructed him to minimize civilian casualties, depriving the enemy of a propaganda issue. The use of fire bombs proved unnecessary that summer, for in mid-September after about one month of systematic bombardment, Stratemeyer announced that practically all the strategic industrial targets in the country had been destroyed by high explosives alone. Since American fighters had wiped out the North Korean air force and the enemy had few antiaircraft guns, B–29 crews could concentrate on accurate bombing. The big problem was weather, for clouds often closed in over the B–29 bases during the course of a mission, and in such conditions, landing was the most dangerous part of the flight.

A Boeing B–29 Superfortress takes off from Japan to bomb a target in Korea.

One of the targets on the list approved by the Joint Chiefs of Staff, Rashin, escaped destruction. Because the town, located in northeastern North Korea, was within 20 miles of Soviet territory, the Department of State insisted that any attack on the oil storage tanks there be carried out in good weather using optical bombsights. The Joint Chiefs of Staff agreed, but word of the requirement for visual aiming failed to reach General O'Donnell. When his B–29s attacked on August 12, they attempted to bomb with radar through a thick overcast but succeeded only in scattering their explosives on the outskirts of town. A second mission, dispatched ten days later after O'Donnell had been reminded of the restriction, found Rashin again hidden by clouds and had to bomb an alternate target. At this point, given the administration's policy of trying to confine fighting to the Korean peninsula, the State Department questioned the wisdom of retaining on the target list a city that close to the Soviet Union. The Joint Chiefs of Staff agreed to its removal, apparently assuming that oil or other cargo shipped through Rashin could be destroyed at some other point during its passage down the eastern coast of Korea. The decision aroused no debate within military circles at the time, although in the late spring of 1951, after China had intervened in the war and MacArthur had been replaced, critics of the Truman administration learned of the immunity given Rashin and denounced the decision as a flagrant example of political interference in military matters. In August 1951, a year after the first raid, with an alarming volume of supplies stockpiled at the city's railyard, Gen. Matthew B. Ridgway, MacArthur's successor, obtained permission from President Truman to bomb Rashin. After waiting for clear skies, B–29s attacked on August 25, dropping 300 tons of bombs, 97 percent of which struck within the rail complex.

While the arguments of Generals Stratemeyer, Weyland, and Vandenberg that the proper missions for the B–29s were long-range interdiction or strategic bombardment resulted in attacks on places like Wonsan and Pyongyang, the danger persisted into August that the North Koreans might mount a massive assault and break through the Pusan perimeter. When the enemy crossed the Naktong River at midmonth and threatened the important road junction of Taegu, General MacArthur summoned Stratemeyer to his office and directed him to carpet bomb an area totaling 27 square miles through which reinforcements and supplies were passing to exploit the Naktong bridgehead. O'Donnell's planners divided the rectangle into 12 squares and dispatched a squadron of B–29s to SATURATE each one with bombs. In less than half an hour on August 16, from an altitude of 10,000 feet, 98 B–29s dropped 960 tons of high explosives, raising blinding clouds of smoke and dust that prevented any sort of damage assessment from the air. Enemy fire from both banks of the river prevented patrols from entering the bombed area, but hostile artillery fire slackened from within the heavily bombed area. Prisoners captured later in the fighting revealed, however, that the bulk of the North Korean force had already crossed the Naktong when the bombs started falling. Despite a lack of immediate intelligence on the results of the August 16 attack, MacArthur wanted to launch a second bombardment on the near shore of the river until dissuaded by his subordinates. Generals Walker, Stratemeyer, and Partridge all insisted that the B–29s be used only against known targets, no matter how serious the emergency; dumping bombs blindly onto the countryside was not likely to do any good.

Joint Operations

During the successful defense of Taegu, fighter-bombers and B–26s did more to check the enemy than did the massive carpet bombing by B–29s. North Korean troops were strafed as they tried to ford the Naktong. Air strikes destroyed underwater bridges built to carry trucks and foot traffic and supported counterattacks against the hostile lodgment east of the stream. Since air power first intervened in Korea, interdiction and close air support by tactical aircraft had helped gain time for the United States to rush troops to the peninsula and stabilize the battlefront there. In support of the early delaying actions, fighter-bombers and light bombers strafed attacking North Korean infantry and destroyed Soviet-built tanks approaching the battlefield or actually firing into American positions. On July 10, for example, a flight of F–80s descended beneath the clouds and discovered a long line of North Korean tanks and trucks halted before a demolished bridge. Responding to the sighting, the Fifth Air Force diverted every available aircraft—80s, B–26s, and even F–82 interceptors—to batter the column with bombs, gunfire, and rockets. This improvisation deprived the advancing enemy of more than 150 badly needed vehicles, a third of them tanks.

To control the entire spectrum of tactical aviation and make sure that bombs and gunfire were delivered when and where they were needed, the Fifth Air Force followed a doctrine that had evolved during World War II but had been modified later to reflect the emergence of the Air Force as a separate service. The principal agency of coordination was the joint operations center, where representatives of the Army and Air Force received requests from the commanders of ground units, matched targets with the available aircraft and ordnance, and used the communications net provided by an Air Force tactical air control center to arrange strikes. Routine requests—for example, strafing and bombing in support of a counterattack the next day—were incorporated into operations orders issued each day; but in an emergency, the center communicated directly with pilots in the vicinity, with the headquarters of ground units, or with nearby airfields. The center launched aircraft or diverted those already aloft to new targets. It did not attempt, however, to control individual strikes but handed the aircraft to a tactical air control officer operating from a radio-equipped jeep and assigned to a particular ground unit. This officer was an experienced pilot familiar with the difficulty of locating a target from the air, with the characteristics of the supporting aircraft, and with the munitions they carried. As a pilot, he was able to communicate with other pilots in language they understood. Such in brief was the mechanism for controlling tactical aviation that Partridge intended to use in Korea.

Problems arose at the outset. Based on experience in World War II, Partridge planned to establish an advance headquarters alongside Walker's command post in Korea, but this could not be done before the North Korean offensive had been slowed, if not stopped. Not until July 24 did the two headquarters begin functioning side by side in the comparative security of Taegu. During the first week of August, however, the enemy threatened even that town, forcing the Eighth Army to move its command post halfway to Pusan. Because the site selected by General Walker was crowded and lacked adequate communications with Japan, the advance headquarters of the Fifth Air Force continued all the way to Pusan.

Meanwhile, Partridge had opened in Korea a joint operations center to take the place of the improvised tactical air control system that had functioned at Suwon until the airfield there was overrun. He placed the center at Taejon, site of the headquarters of the first American infantry division sent to the peninsula. At the time, mid-July, the division was so desperate for officers in its battalions that none could be assigned permanently to the joint operations center, although the staff sections did share information with the airmen. When the North Koreans overwhelmed Taejon, the center shifted to Taegu, remaining there after higher headquarters had left the town.

While the joint operations center was being set up in Korea, the Fifth Air Force sent a handful of radio-equipped jeeps to the peninsula for use by forward air controllers. To call in a strike, however, the control parties had to drive far enough forward to see the target, for the radios were too heavy to carry and lacked the equipment for remote transmission. Since the sight of a jeep on the skyline was an invitation for the enemy to open fire, the tactical air control parties sustained heavy losses during the early fighting. To replace them, the Fifth Air Force turned to airborne controllers in light aircraft. When these observation craft proved easy prey for propeller-driven North Korean fighters, the North American T–6 trainer, known as the AT–6 during World War II, was pressed into service as a vehicle for forward air controllers. This aircraft had the speed to escape the Soviet-built Yaks and the maneuverability to enable the controller to peer beyond ridge lines into valleys hidden from a control party on the ground. The Mosquitoes, as the controllers in the T–6s were called, came to provide the principal means of controlling close-in air strikes, eclipsing the jeep-mounted control parties that had been so successful during World War II.

A further complication not experienced by tactical airmen during the liberation of Europe was partnership with the Navy and Marine Corps. Difficulties began on July 4, when Admiral Struble continued for a second day his carrier-based attacks on Pyongyang. Before the previous day's bombing, the commander of Task Force 77 had advised Admiral Joy of the planned attacks at Haeju and Pyongyang, and Joy passed the information to Stratemeyer, who asked only that the naval aircraft confine activity on July 3 to the vicinity of the capital and leave the rest of the peninsula to the Fifth Air Force. Struble, however, decided on his own to hit Pyongyang again, a decision that compelled Stratemeyer to cancel a B–29 strike planned for that city on the same day. The incident convinced the Air Force general that he needed tighter control over air strikes by the Navy, especially those that might be delivered against targets close to the front lines. Stratemeyer therefore asked MacArthur for operational control over the Navy's carrier aircraft, in effect assigning them a status similar to the squadrons of the Fifth Air Force. Admiral Joy objected on doctrinal as well as practical grounds. He did not believe that the recent agreements on roles and missions would permit another service to exercise direct control over naval aviation, especially when operating at sea, or that the joint operations center could maintain adequate control of Navy as well as Air Force aircraft. From the Navy's point of view, the joint operations center seemed best suited to aerial operations scheduled in advance and spread over a wide front. Granted that the center could juggle assigned aircraft in an emergency, doubt persisted among naval aviators that it could

General Douglas MacArthur (*second from left*) visits an air base in Korea: Maj. Gen. Earle E. Partridge, commander of Fifth Air Force, is second from the right.

funnel any large number of strikes into a small area without overloading its communications channels. Although he wanted no part of Air Force control and remained wary of the joint operations center, Admiral Joy recognized the need for closer coordination of tactical aviation. Consequently, on July 15 he agreed to place the carrier aircraft under the "coordination control" of the Far East Air Forces, an ill-defined arrangement under which he did little more than provide Stratemeyer's headquarters with Admiral Struble's plans for carrier strikes. He thus avoided Air Force control, but naval aircraft approaching the battlefield had to report to the joint operations center for assignment to a Mosquito controller.

Some of the Navy's fears concerning the joint operations center proved justified. The volume of radio traffic at times inundated the system, and important messages intended for Task Force 77 sometimes failed to arrive in time. Moreover, the job of handling close air support by naval aircraft fell to already overburdened controllers, who might be trying to meld F–80 fighter-bombers, based in Japan and already short of fuel, with longer range, propeller-driven attack planes that despite their greater endurance had to return to their carriers and land before dark.

After this shaky beginning, cooperation improved. The carriers tried to send a more even flow of aircraft over the battlefront, and naval airborne controllers in Douglas attack aircraft joined the Air Force controllers in T–6s to direct air strikes. Not until 1951, however, did Task Force 77 send pilots to the joint operations center on a regular basis as liaison officers, and the establishment of direct communications between the center and the task force was similarly delayed. The war was within a month of ending before the Navy in 1953 allowed its representative at the joint operations center to make binding commitments on targets and sorties.

Meanwhile, centralized control of tactical aviation as prescribed in Air Force doctrine had also been challenged by the arrival early in August 1950 of a Marine brigade and its supporting aircraft group. The Marine Corps believed that its ground units, whether regiments, a hurriedly formed brigade like the one sent to Korea, or divisions, should operate in conjunction with an aircraft group or, in the case of a division, an aircraft wing. Because of the nature of amphibious warfare in which the marines specialized—a small beachhead seized with the help of naval gunfire and air support and then expanded to accommodate artillery—Marine Corps airmen had extensive training in the close support of infantry. Pilots, air controllers, and commanders on the ground were accustomed to working together and understood the benefits and dangers of air strikes in close proximity to friendly troops. Whereas Marine Corps aviation thought in terms of supporting Marine ground units fighting on a comparatively narrow front, the Air Force in Korea employed aircraft for interdiction, reconnaissance, and close air support from the Pusan perimeter near the southern tip of the peninsula to the Yalu River in the North and from one end of the battleline to the other. In terms of interest and training—lose air support had a lower priority in the Air Force than in the Marine Corps—as well as geographic concentration, Marine Corps pilots supported ground forces better than their Air Force counterparts. Because the skills of Marine airmen were so highly prized, General Partridge sought close cooperation with the Marine squadrons, which at first were flying missions from aircraft carriers off the South Korean coast. He requested and received a liaison officer from the aircraft group who helped the joint operations center find suitable targets for any

Marine strike aircraft that were surplus to the needs of the brigade.

To the annoyance of Generals Stratemeyer and Vandenberg, the American press lavished praise on Marine airmen for doing an excellent job of close air support, as indeed they were, albeit on a comparatively small scale. However skilled these first Marine Corps pilots to fight in Korea were in their specialty of close air support, they could not by themselves maintain control of the skies over the peninsula or carry the weight of ordnance delivered by the much larger Fifth Air Force over a much larger area. Like close air support, interdiction contributed to the defense of the Pusan perimeter, sometimes spectacularly, as when a motorized column went up in flames, at other times all but invisibly, as when downed bridges delayed the arrival of badly needed ammunition or reinforcements. General Walker, moreover, expressed satisfaction with the work of the Air Force, declaring: "I will lay my cards right on the table and state that if it had not been for the air support we received from the Fifth Air Force we would not have been able to stay in Korea."

From Inchon to Pyongyang

By mid-September the North Korean offensive had clearly failed; the United Nations forces had survived savage blows and grown steadily stronger. The first phase of the Korean fighting had ended. MacArthur's belief, expressed to Partridge in the early days of the conflict, that American air power would prevail, turned out to be mistaken. Fighting the North Koreans to a standstill required the combined efforts of the air, land, and sea forces of several nations, with South Korea and the United States making the greatest contributions. Air power did, however, provide essential help as the United Nations Command stopped the enemy drive. The burned-out hulks of hundreds of tanks destroyed by air strikes marked the invasion route, and B–29s had damaged the North Korean transportation network and destroyed whatever industry the nation possessed. Although handicapped by primitive airfields in South Korea, the Combat Cargo Command of Far East Air Forces flew in men and cargo from Japan and evacuated almost a third of the 13,000 American soldiers sent to Japan to recuperate from their wounds. The Military Air Transport Service flew the transpacific routes, delivering among other things a new and more powerful rocket launcher used by American infantrymen against North Korean tanks in the fight for Taejon during mid-July. In addition, the transport service conducted weather reconnaissance, provided weather forecasts for use by the Army and Air Force, and dispatched rescue detachments that served under the operational control of the Far East Air Forces. The Air Force had drawn heavily on the experience of the Army Air Forces in helping check the advance of a North Korean army that fought with the weapons and tactics of World War II. Establishing the Pusan perimeter was just the beginning, however; as early as the first week of July, MacArthur had been thinking of employing the basic tactics that had served him so well against the Japanese in the South Pacific. He ordered that planning begin for an amphibious landing in Korea well beyond the battlefront.

The objective that MacArthur selected to open the second phase of the war was Inchon on Korea's west coast, the ocean gateway to Seoul. His amphibious spearhead was the 1st Marine Division, which absorbed the brigade that had fought to defend the Pusan perimeter. MacArthur placed his chief of staff, General Almond, in command of the 40,000-man invasion force, designated X Corps, which included the marines and an Army division from Japan. The attack at Inchon cut off the North Korean forces retreating from the Pusan perimeter, where the Eighth Army launched its own offensive on September 16, the day following the assault at Inchon. Less than a third of a North Korean force numbering 100,000 escaped from the trap and again crossed the 38th parallel, this time in headlong retreat. So complete was the enemy's collapse that on September 27, not quite two weeks after the Inchon landing, President Truman authorized MacArthur to pursue the beaten enemy north of the parallel separating the two Koreas, and South Korean troops promptly advanced into the North. The United Nations never explicitly approved an invasion of North Korea, however. The General Assembly, reflecting the concern of some members that to advance northward was to invite the Chinese to intervene, adopted an ambiguous compromise resolution to the effect that "all appropriate steps should be taken to ensure conditions of stability throughout Korea."

As the United Nations forces advanced beyond the 38th parallel, air power performed a variety of missions. Navy and Marine Corps aviators had provided cover for the Inchon landings, while the Fifth Air Force supported the Eighth Army throughout the advance from the Pusan perimeter to the border with North Korea. Once across the parallel, easily the most spectacular air operation was the dropping of the 187th Airborne Regimental Combat Team at two road junctions north of Pyongyang to cut off a retreating North Korean column and free a large number of American prisoners of war traveling with it in two trains. A sharp fight occurred, but the sudden appearance of the airborne force did not prevent the enemy from murdering a hundred prisoners on one of the trains; the other continued northward with its captives. Besides dropping the airborne infantry, the roughly 140 transport aircraft of the Far East Air Forces parachuted supplies to the advancing United Nations troops and flew men and cargo—as much as 1,000 passengers and 1,000 tons of supplies on a busy day—from Japan to airfields in Korea. With the North Korean People's Army straggling in small groups into the northern mountains of Korea and town after town falling to Walker's advancing army,

For a short time in the fall of 1950, Fifth Air Force made its headquarters here in Pyongyang, the North Korean capital. Soon a Chinese offensive would force American units to scramble southward.

few worthwhile targets existed for the fighter-bombers of the Fifth Air Force or for O'Donnell's B–29s. Aerial reconnaissance, so helpful in charting the defenses of Inchon, now faced the infinitely more difficult task of locating the enemy among the mountains of northernmost Korea.

The advance that carried the Eighth Army to Pyongyang and beyond formed one arm of another pincers movement, planned as a repetition of the assault at Inchon. While the Eighth Army pushed northward, General Almond's X Corps would reembark at Inchon and Pusan, sail around the peninsula, and land at Wonsan on the east coast. Once ashore it would cross the mountainous spine of Korea to link up with the main body of the Eighth Army at Korea's narrow waist. The plan went badly awry, however. While resistance before the Eighth Army was crumbling, minefields off Wonsan delayed the landing of X Corps for two weeks; Almond's troops did not come ashore until November 4, after South Korean forces advancing along the coast had captured the port. The planned pincers movement now became a race to the northern border of North Korea, the Yalu River, by parallel columns with a rugged mountain range between them.

The separation of the Eighth Army and the X Corps, which still included the 1st Marine Division, brought about a change in the relationship between the Fifth Air Force and Marine Corps aviation, which had been reinforced to become the 1st Marine Aircraft Wing. In October, General Weyland, still serving as Stratemeyer's vice commander for operations, raised the question whether the Marine aircraft wing, when supporting X Corps in northeastern North Korea, would come under the control of the Fifth Air Force. Initially MacArthur's headquarters said no, apparently intending to repeat at Wonsan the arrangement at Inchon, where Marine Corps and Navy squadrons supported the landing. Weyland thereupon argued that the Fifth Air Force was responsible for supporting X Corps and should control the Marine Corps aircraft, which would operate from bases ashore during the advance to the Yalu. He proposed that Partridge extend his coordination control over the 1st Marine Aircraft Wing, agreeing, however, to commit the wing primarily to the support of X Corp and to provide from the Fifth Air Force any additional sorties that Almond's command might require. During the final advance by the United Nations Command to the Yalu, the Navy's carrier-based aircraft, like the B–29s of the Far East Air Forces, would conduct general support. On October 16, when the first elements of X Corps set sail for Wonsan, MacArthur's headquarters approved the arrangement, which went into effect five days later as the amphibious force was steaming offshore, waiting for the minefields to be cleared.

The plan to have the Fifth Air Force exercise coordination control over the Marines did not work as well as Weyland had hoped. Communications between the joint operations center and the X Corps command post proved unreliable, and Almond declined to assign officers to the center on a permanent basis. Partridge imposed a further burden on the fragile communications net by insisting that X Corps submit each day a formal request for air strikes; this long and complicated message became the basis for a detailed order directing the 1st Marine Aircraft Wing to fly missions that it would have flown anyway. According to Robert Frank Futrell's history of the Air Force in Korea, this procedure "represented an unrealistic compliance with accepted air-ground doctrine." In the middle of October, resistance in northeastern Korea was light, and the cumbersome exchange of messages amounted to little more than an inconvenience. At the end of November, however, China intervened in force, attacking the troops advancing from Wonsan and those pushing toward the Yalu after capturing Pyongyang, ending the pursuit of the defeated North Korean army that had begun on September 15 and 16 with the landing at Inchon and the counterattack from the Pusan perimeter.

Chinese Intervention

The Chinese intervention jolted a United Nations Command that already had begun canceling requisitions for ammunition and clearly was thinking of victory parades rather than further combat. Indeed, two of the five groups of B–29s assigned to Far East Air Forces returned to the United States in October. On the 15th of that month, before the Wonsan invasion force had left port, General MacArthur arrived at Wake Island where he assured President Truman that "if the Chinese tried to get down to Pyongyang there would be the greatest slaughter." China had threatened to enter the war if the United Nations forces drew too near to the Yalu, but these warnings were dismissed as propaganda. Not even the sighting on October 18 of 100 fighters parked on the airfield at An-tung (now romanized as Dandong) in Manchuria caused alarm; Stratemeyer interpreted their presence as an attempt to lend "color and credence to menacing statements and threats of Chinese communist leaders, who probably felt that this display of strength involved no risk in view of our apparent desire to avoid border incidents."

When the Chinese struck, they attacked piecemeal. On October 25 and 26, they hit South Korean troops who had probed as far as the Yalu, and on the 29th the South Koreans who had captured Wonsan reported encountering Chinese troops along the east coast. Other more serious contacts occurred on November 1. When F–80s attacked the airfield at Sinuiju on the southern bank of the Yalu, they found 15 Yaks on the ground there and lost one of their number to antiaircraft fire, some of it believed to have come from An-tung across the border in Manchuria. On that same day, also in the vicinity of Sinuiju, Yak fighters of a reconstituted North Korean air arm attacked a B–26 and a T–6 but failed to down either, and four MiG–15 jet fighters bearing Chinese markings darted across the Yalu and jumped four F–51s, all of which escaped. When night fell at Unsan, some 75 miles east of Sinuiju, Chinese infantry attacked both American and South Korean units, inflicting severe casualties. The Chinese were not merely reinforcing the defeated North Koreans but were taking over the war. Instead of some 17,000 troops, as MacArthur's staff believed, as many as 180,000 had already entered North Korea, traveling by night when American aerial reconnaissance could not detect them and remaining hidden during daylight.

American attention focused on Sinuiju, the bridges there, and the other spans that crossed the Yalu elsewhere. Partridge wanted to avenge the loss of the F–80 on November 1 by setting the town ablaze with incendiary bombs, chasing back into Manchuria any Chinese MiGs that might intervene, and attacking the airfields from which the Chinese jets had come. Until the extent of the Chinese involvement became clear, MacArthur was reluctant to challenge the administration's prohibition against attacking China, and he vetoed the bombing of Sinuiju, which he hoped to capture intact and turn over to the government of a unified Korea. With a peacetime population ap-

F–51 Mustang pilots await debriefing after attacking Chinese forces near Seoul, South Korea.

proaching 100,000, many of whom had fled across the Yalu, the town would serve as the anchor of a defensive line established along the river.

Even as he sought to spare Sinuiju for use by the new Korea's armed forces, MacArthur approved the destruction by aerial bombardment of the other towns and villages in the border region that might harbor enemy troops or supplies. To compensate for the withdrawal of the two groups of B–29s, O'Donnell's bomber command relied on incendiaries to multiply the damage done by the remaining three groups. The administration apparently was no longer concerned by the propaganda advantage that might accrue to the government of North Korea if fire bombs were used. During the first week of November, the bombers ignored Sinuiju in the west and Rashin in the east but hit the other two large towns in the border region, leveling Kangye and damaging Chonjin.

Although still confident that he faced a comparatively small number of Chinese, MacArthur could not ignore the passage of additional troops over the bridges linking China with North Korea. On November 5 he therefore directed Stratemeyer to devastate the area between the front lines and the Yalu River, attacking the town of Sinuiju, dropping the "Korean end" of all the bridges leading from Manchuria, and then destroying every village, town, factory, or military installation, exempting only Rashin and the hydroelectric plants that supplied current to China. Sent in a routine targeting report filed a few hours before the B–29s were to take off on the first of the missions, the directive might have gone unnoticed until after the first strike had Stratemeyer not alerted Vandenberg that stray bombs aimed at Sinuiju or the bridges might explode on Chinese territory. The issue reached the desk of President Truman, who felt an attack like this should be delivered only if the lives of American soldiers were at stake. Thus far, the Chief Executive had received no such justification. MacArthur was therefore asked why the series of operations was suddenly so important. He responded by giving the Joint Chiefs of Staff a vivid description of Chinese troops pouring across the bridges in days to come. To delay the bombing, he warned, would threaten the "ultimate destruction of the forces under my command." Despite the possibility of provoking China into broadening the conflict, perhaps by a move against Taiwan, the President felt he had no choice but to approve the strikes against Sinuiju and the bridges.

On November 8, 79 B–29s struck Sinuiju, nine trying unsuccessfully to drop the bridges and the other 70 saturating the city with more than 500 tons of incendiary bombs, released in clusters. "General O'Donnell indicates," Stratemeyer recorded in his diary, "that the town was gone." Aerial reconnaissance found that about 60 percent of the city had been destroyed. No B–29s were lost on the raid against Sinuiju and its bridges, and 1st Lt. Russell Brown, flying cover in an F–80, shot down a MiG–15 during the first all-jet dogfight. Enemy antiaircraft artillery kept the B–29s above 18,000 feet, an altitude that made it impossible to hit the Korean end of the two bridges, highway and railroad, between An-tung and Sinuiju. A further complication was MacArthur's insistence that the bombers follow the course of the stream to avoid violating Chinese airspace. At day's end both bridges remained open, although the approaches from the Korean side had sustained damage.

Throughout the rest of November 1950, the dozen bridges over the Yalu proved to be durable targets. Navy aircraft managed to destroy the highway span at Sinuiju, but seven other structures, including the railroad bridge at Sinuiju, defied all efforts to destroy them, even with radio-controlled bombs, relics of World War II that had a guidance system prone to failure. Few B–29 bombardiers had any experience using the bombs, which they had to track all the way to the target, disregarding MiGs and antiaircraft fire. Even if greater accuracy had been attained, the 1,000-pound guided bombs lacked the explosive power to destroy these solidly built bridges. Before heavier guided bombs could be sent to the Far East and crews trained to use them, the Yalu froze, enabling men and supplies to cross without using the bridges. One of the first of the 12,000-pound guided bombs to arrive in the theater of operations badly damaged a railroad bridge at Kangye, some 25 miles inside North Korea. In March, after the ice had thawed, the B–29s resumed their attacks on the bridges across the Yalu, damaging a few but not the railroad span at Sinuiju.

During the early strikes against the Yalu bridges, fighters from north of the river frequently climbed to high altitude over Manchuria, dived into North Korea to make a firing pass at the American bombers, and then fled back across the border. MacArthur complained about allowing the enemy to enjoy this Manchurian sanctuary, but the possibility that aerial incursions north of the border might trigger a violent response by China or the Soviet Union had become a source of concern to America's European allies. American aircraft had already violated Chinese or Soviet airspace three times: on August 27, two Mustangs had mistaken an airfield at An-tung for one at Sinuiju and strafed the Chinese aerodrome; on the night of September 22, a B–29 dispatched to bomb Sinuiju hit the railyard at An-tung; and on October 8, two F–80 pilots became lost and repeatedly strafed a Soviet air base in Siberia. Violations of communist air space were considered potentially dangerous provocations of an enemy whose intentions were not yet clear. A Chinese protest on August 28, which alleged five incursions, moved General Stratemeyer to warn Partridge and O'Donnell that intervention was a "distinct possibility," but the American advance continued and soon the concerns of the late summer were forgotten. After the attack on Soviet territory, the commander of the fighter group involved was reassigned to Fifth

Air Force headquarters and the offending pilots faced a court-martial that acquitted them.

Since the extent of Chinese involvement in Korea was only gradually becoming understood, the United States agreed with its allies that extending the air war beyond the Yalu would be unwise, especially in light of rumors that the Soviet Air Force would respond to American attacks against airfields in China. The Truman administration, although it almost certainly would have retaliated against the air bases had the Chinese mounted an aerial attack on the United Nations forces, did not want to provoke raids of that kind. Never during the war were American flyers authorized to enter Chinese or Soviet airspace. Pilots sometimes ignored this prohibition when in hot pursuit of a MiG seeking refuge over China, and on at least one occasion they confused facilities across the Soviet border with targets in North Korea.

After the first attacks by Chinese troops in late October and early November, quiet settled over the North Korean battlefields; the new enemy seemed to have vanished as suddenly as he appeared. After pausing two weeks to regroup, MacArthur on November 24 launched an offensive that he believed would drive the enemy across the Yalu and into China. He was confident that the United Nations Command could rout the Chinese, now estimated to number about 70,000, and the slightly larger remnant of the North Korean People's Army. In fact, some

Marshal Peng Dehuai commanded Chinese forces during the Korean War.

300,000 Chinese, along with the defeated North Koreans, opposed a United Nations force of 200,000 men, half of them South Korean troops.

The Chinese counterattacked on November 25, striking the main body of the Eighth Army and then X Corps. After four days, MacArthur ordered the forces north of Pyongyang to withdraw, although he hoped that Almond could maintain a salient in the flank of the advancing enemy. Marine Corps aviation and the Navy's carrier task force concentrated on assisting the troops in the northeast, who were falling back on Hungnam, a port about fifty miles north of Wonsan. In the emergency, Partridge suspended the existing procedures for coordination and allowed the commander of the 1st Marine Aircraft Wing to direct air operations in that sector, acting independently of the joint operations center. In addition, the Fifth Air Force placed varying numbers of sorties by fighter-bombers and light bombers at the disposal of the Marine Corps officer. Partridge's remaining aircraft, aided by the B–29s, tried to relieve the pressure on General Walker's Eighth Army. Commanded by Maj. Gen. William H. Tunner, who had directed the recent Berlin Airlift, the combat cargo element of the Far East Air Forces flew into airfields that were about to be abandoned in the retreat and brought out equipment and supplies that Walker's troops would otherwise have had to destroy. Along the east coast, Tunner's airmen parachuted the components of a bridge that, when assembled, enabled the 1st Marine Division to cross a gorge blocking the line of retreat to Hungnam. Without the bridge, the unit might well have lost much of its heavy equipment. After a gallant fight to reach the port, Hungnam had to be abandoned, with the last of Almond's troops sailing safely from the harbor on December 24. The presence of the marines and soldiers on the Chinese flank no longer made sense; they were needed in South Korea to stabilize the front as United Nations forces abandoned Pyongyang, retreated across the 38th parallel, and abandoned Seoul. Each successive retreat further complicated tactical air support by depriving Partridge of his advance airfields and reducing the time that fighter-bombers could harry the enemy's advance.

The bleak news from Korea deeply troubled President Truman and his advisers. After a meeting at the White House on November 28, when the Chinese offensive was just beginning, the danger of sustained air attacks from the sanctuary of Manchuria was discussed. The possibility of retaliation in the event of such attacks was very much on the President's mind, so much so that during a press conference on November 30, he answered a reporter's question about the use of atomic bombs by stating that there had "always been active consideration" of their employment. This offhand remark, though clarified by a White House press release pointing out that the President had not authorized the use of atomic devices and that only when he did so would MacArthur "have charge of the tactical delivery of the weapons," produced two immediate effects. General MacArthur, who had just approved a message requesting B–29s capable of dropping atomic bombs, set his headquarters to work on a list of potential targets in China and, should the conflict spread, in the Soviet Union. At the same time, Mr. Truman's words upset America's allies in the North Atlantic Treaty Organization, who initially supported the collective defense of South Korea as proof of American determination to abandon isolationism and participate in the defense of nations threatened by communist aggression. The enthusiasm of the Europeans was fast abating, for they feared that the war in Korea might at best absorb American resources needed by the North Atlantic Treaty Organization or at worst give the Soviet Union an excuse to attack western Europe. Prime Minister Clement H. Atlee of Great Britain flew to Washington seeking reassurance; the President provided it, telling of his hope "that world conditions would never call for the use of the atomic bomb."

MiG Alley

While MacArthur planned, albeit tentatively, for atomic warfare and Truman responded to the concerns of the European leaders who recoiled at the prospect of such a conflict, the Air Force moved to solve a tactical problem, countering the Soviet-built MiG–15, which in terms of speed and maneuverability outperformed the F–51s and F–80s in action over Korea. Even as the Chinese drive gathered momentum, the Fifth Air Force received an aircraft, the North American F–86 Sabre, that more than matched the MiG–15 in performance. Soon after Chinese MiGs (manned in the earliest days by Soviet pilots) first intervened in the air war, General Vandenberg ordered a wing of seventy-five Sabres ferried by aircraft carrier to the Far East. They had their first encounter with the MiG–15 on December 17, 1950, when Lt. Col. Bruce Hinton shot one down. Five days later, the commander of the 4th Fighter-Interceptor Wing, Lt. Col. John C. Meyer, led eight Sabres against fifteen MiGs, downing six of the enemy at the cost of one F–86.

During the next 30 months, F–86 pilots received credit for the destruction of 792 MiGs and 18 other enemy aircraft. Of the 218 Sabres lost during the war, the Air Force attributed 76 to MiGs, 19 to ground fire, 15 to unknown enemy action, 13 to unknown operational causes, and the rest to mechanical failure or accident. Although the lighter MiG could climb faster, the Sabre could outrun it in a dive and was more responsive to the controls when approaching the speed of sound. The Sabre's canopy afforded better visibility than that of the MiG, which suffered from a restricted field of vision and an inferior defrosting system. Neither aircraft had really adequate armament. The Sabre's six machine guns did not cause enough damage, often hitting the enemy without bringing him down, and the MiG's cannon fired too slowly to be accurate against a fast-moving jet. Modifications to the F–86 enhanced its performance against the MiG, which did not improve much during the course of the war. To reduce drag during tight turns, engineers at North American Aviation replaced the wing slats that extended automatically at low speed with a fixed leading edge. Hydraulic controls also increased agility, but the greatest boon to maneuverability was the so-called flying tail, a horizontal stabilizer that moved as a unit and was far more effective than the smaller elevators on the early F–86. A more powerful engine and a radar gunsight also helped make the later F–86 a more formidable fighter. The MiG, however, still had better acceleration and enjoyed the sanctuary of the Manchurian border.

Although the F–86 was a splendid fighter, its overwhelming success against the MiG in Korea resulted in large measure from its superior pilots, many of them veterans of World War II. Colonel Meyer, for example, was a leading ace in the European Theater of Operations with twenty-four kills; he added two victories in Korea. Similarly, Lt. Col. Francis Gabreski and seventeen other aces of the previous war increased their totals in the Korean fighting. Ten men who had at least a few victories in World War II became aces in Korea, including Maj.

An Air Force ground crew "unwraps" a North American F–86 Sabre on a cold winter day in Korea; this F–86 will soon fly north hunting for Chinese MiG–15s.

Maj. Frederick "Boots" Blesse was one of thirty-eight USAF pilots to become a Korean War "ace" by shooting down at least five enemy aircraft. Here he is shown in 1952 with eight stars on his F–86 indicating eight victories; he will get two more. Soon after the war, Blesse published his pioneering essay on jet air-to-air tactics: "No Guts, No Glory." He retired from the Air Force in 1975 as a major general.

James Jabara, whose fifteen kills earned him second place among the aces of the Korean War. The leading ace, with sixteen, was Capt. Joseph McConnell, who had been a B–24 navigator during World War II. He survived the air war over Korea only to die while testing a new model of the F–86. Against experienced pilots like Gabreski, Meyer, and Jabara, the Chinese sent class after class of trainees, and the Soviets also rotated inexperienced pilots into the theater. Each group began timidly and only gradually made bolder forays across the Yalu as experience increased. Only a few of the Chinese and Soviet pilots attained the level of skill common among their opponents.

The F–86 pilots had to devise new tactics for jet combat along the Yalu. The big offensive fighter sweeps of the last years of World War II gave way to small defensive patrols. Since the Manchurian airfields could not be attacked, the F–86s did not engage the enemy over his bases as had been done in both World Wars. The initiative thus passed to the Chinese, with the Americans reacting to the enemy's incursions by establishing barrier patrols or by scrambling interceptors when warned by radar. Because of the short range of the MiG–15 and the location of the Chinese airfields it used, the heaviest fighting took place in "MiG Alley," in northwestern North Korea along the Yalu River from the Yellow Sea to the Sui-ho Reservoir, an area that included the towns of Sinanju and Sinuiju. The short range of the F–86, less than 500 miles with jettisonable fuel tanks, meant that no time could be wasted in assembling large formations. Patrols of four F–86s arrived in MiG Alley at five-minute intervals and remained for about 20 minutes, less if they engaged in combat.

Although American tactics proved successful, Chinese air power remained an ominous threat throughout the fighting. Soviet support had enabled China to increase its jet fighter strength to as many as 1,000 aircraft, three times the peak number of F–86s. MiGs occasionally penetrated the screen of F–86s along the Yalu, and U.S. fighter protection disappeared entirely for several weeks. Early in 1951, the United Nations forces abandoned Seoul; and on January 2, about to be deprived of Kimpo airfield just outside the capital, the F–86s withdrew to Japan. Not until they returned to South Korea in February could the Sabres again reach MiG Alley; but in the interim, American bombers and fighter-bombers (including new Repub-

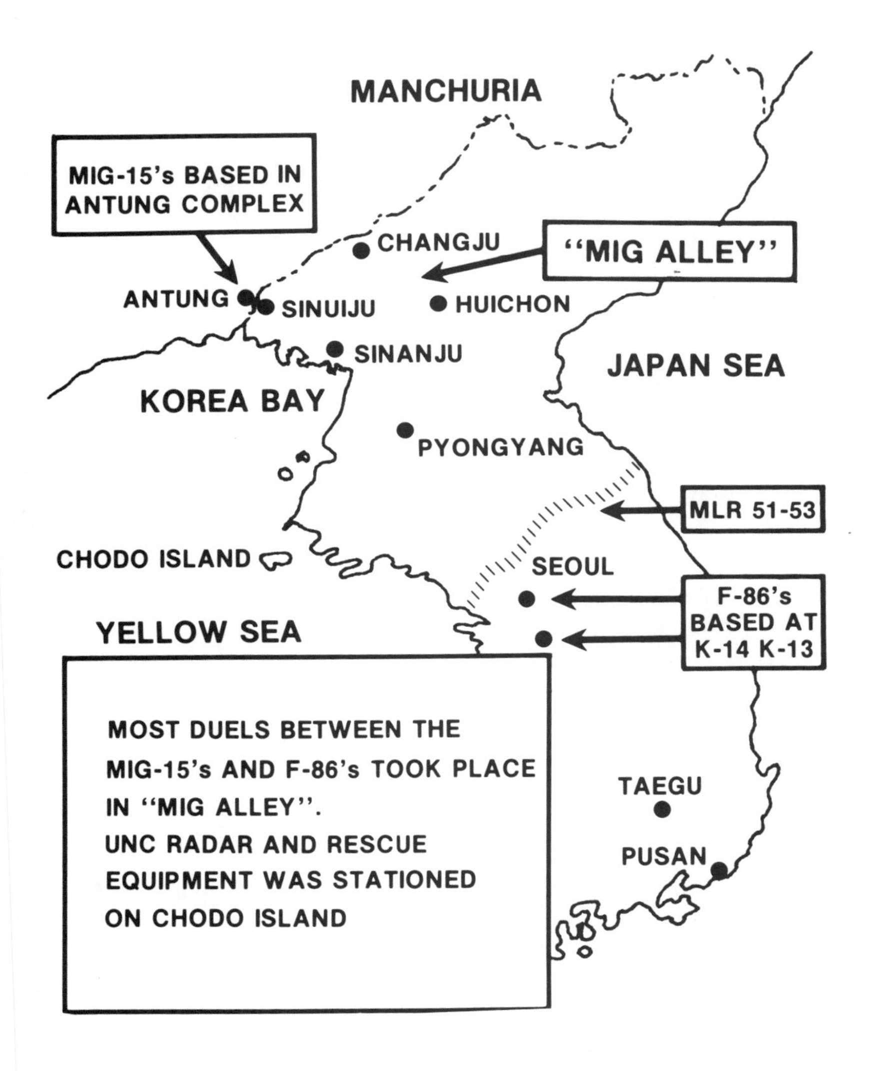
MANCHURIA
MIG-15's BASED IN ANTUNG COMPLEX
CHANGJU
"MIG ALLEY"
ANTUNG
SINUIJU
HUICHON
SINANJU
JAPAN SEA
KOREA BAY
PYONGYANG
MLR 51-53
CHODO ISLAND
SEOUL
F-86's BASED AT K-14 K-13
YELLOW SEA
MOST DUELS BETWEEN THE MIG-15's AND F-86's TOOK PLACE IN "MIG ALLEY".
UNC RADAR AND RESCUE EQUIPMENT WAS STATIONED ON CHODO ISLAND
TAEGU
PUSAN

lic F–74 Thunderjets) achieved varying degrees of success pounding the enemy and his lengthening supply lines without the F–86 screen. B–29s cratered Pyongyang airfield after the enemy recaptured it and bombed towns suspected of sheltering Chinese troops. In January a raid on the city of Pyongyang set raging fires but failed to inflict the complete devastation that the bomber command expected. More encouraging results were attributed to tactical aircraft. During the first five days of January, the Fifth Air Force claimed that some 2,500 daylight sorties by fighter-bombers had killed 8,000 Chinese, while B–26s, experimenting with flares provided by the Navy and dropped from Air Force C–47s, added to the death toll with night attacks.

All in all, air support during the retreat was uneven, weakest in the west during December, when airfields like those around Pyongyang had to be abandoned and mountains of supplies and equipment destroyed, but more effective in the east where aircraft carriers were close at hand and the evacuation more orderly. Once Marine Corps and Air Force fighter-bomber units reestablished themselves in southern South Korea in early January, they launched fiercer attacks than during the previous month. B–29s remained a powerful element in the American air armada because the recently evacuated airfields of North Korea were in no condition for use by MiGs, whose short range kept them well to the north of retreating United Nations forces.

Stalemate

The cumulative effect of attacks on the enemy's logistics network, which intensified as December ended and January began; stiffening resistance on the ground, to which close air support and battlefield interdiction contributed; and the very speed of an advance that outran its supply lines combined to slow the Chinese advance beyond Seoul. By mid-January the long retreat had ended. The front stabilized some forty miles south of the South Korean capital, and the Eighth Army prepared to counterattack under a new commander, Lt. Gen. Matthew B. Ridgway, who had taken over after General Walker died in a jeep accident on December 23, 1950. Ready to take part in

Ridgway's planned advance was X Corps, which had rejoined Eighth Army after the withdrawal from Hungnam.

Since X Corps had returned to the battlefield in South Korea, Partridge might have vigorously reasserted coordination control over the 1st Marine Aircraft Wing through the joint operations center, but he did not. As a result of the savage fighting in northeastern Korea, he recognized that the Marine Corps air and ground components formed a unified team. He therefore continued the practice he had established during the retreat to Hungnam, exercising his authority through the commander of the Marine aircraft wing, with the operations center rarely making other than minor adjustments to plans submitted by wing headquarters. In an emergency Marine Corps aircraft could be directed to attack wherever they were needed, but because Ridgway chose to advance methodically in successive stages, emergencies were few. Indeed, by the end of June the Eighth Army had recaptured Seoul and advanced a short distance into North Korea. The war thereupon entered a new phase, a stalemate broken by limited though vicious attacks, which lasted into 1953.

Air power proved invaluable in the limited United Nations offensives that established an essentially permanent battlefront generally along the 38th parallel north of Seoul. As the United Nations Command fought its way northward, the Far East Air Forces flew as many as 1,000 sorties in a single day. Marine Corps airmen joined them in close air support, under the direction of airborne controllers, and in battlefield interdiction. In terrain that was more open than along the Yalu, aerial reconnaissance kept track of hostile activity, for instance, reporting the enemy's withdrawal from Chunchon just south of the 38th parallel, thus facilitating the advance. B–29s of the Far East Air Forces bombed the road and rail junctions through which supplies reached the Chinese and North Korean units, and troop carrier squadrons dropped the 187th Airborne Regimental Combat Team in the vicinity of Munsan-ni, some 25 miles northwest of Seoul. Assessing the effectiveness of air power in front of his unit, especially the strikes handled by airborne controllers in their T–6s, Lt. Col. Gilbert J. Check, commander of the 27th Regimental Combat Team, said, "The close support and coordination between air and ground units . . . can well serve as a standard for future operations."

The Chinese intervention struck a mortal blow to the administration's lingering hope that the budget could be balanced by reining in defense spending. Amid the optimism of late October, plans were being made to shift troops from the Far East to Europe once the last spark of North Korean resistance had been extinguished. The offensive designed to accomplish this goal began in late November. "If successful," MacArthur declared, "this should for all practical purposes end the war." Scarcely had he spoken before the United Nations Command was everywhere retreating before a massive and well-trained Chinese army. On December 15, President Truman declared a national emergency, committing the United States to the expense of a continuing military buildup.

This marshaling of men and resources, however, was directed as much toward the defense of Europe as toward the war in Asia, for the Chinese offensive had persuaded the administration to settle for less than victory in Korea. To launch another drive to the Yalu against Chinese forces seemed far too costly, not only in terms of American lives lost but also because it would require troops and equipment that could better be used to bolster the defenses of a more vital region, western Europe. Preserving the independence of South Korea without allowing the conflict to spread replaced the defeat of North Korea as the aim of the war. By the time the United Nations troops had begun counterattacking after halting the Chinese advance, the destruction of the enemy's army seemed prohibitively expensive. A better solution appeared to be a negotiated settlement that would end the fighting and ensure the continued independence of South Korea.

General MacArthur, however, would accept nothing less than victory. His concern that the Eighth Army would have to evacuate the peninsula vanished by mid-February, and he denounced the acceptance of a stalemate in Korea. By mid-March, after Ridgway's troops had dealt the Chinese several sharp blows, MacArthur told reporters that the mission of his command was to unify the two Koreas. Although the President in the discouraging days following China's intervention had issued a directive warning against unauthorized statements on the conduct of the war, MacArthur received no rebuke. Since Ridgway's Eighth Army was approaching the 38th parallel, Truman hoped to capitalize on the reversal of Chinese fortunes, and possibly forestall an enemy counterthrust, by offering to negotiate an end to the fighting. Learning in advance of the President's plan, MacArthur torpedoed it, issuing a ringing declaration that in effect invited China to choose between surrender and defeat. On March 24, Truman reminded the general of the directive against public statements on the conduct of the war, but by that time MacArthur had engaged in an even more serious act of insubordination. Four days earlier he had replied to a request from Representative Joe Martin, a Republican from Pennsylvania, for his views on the military policy of the Democratic administration. On April 5 Martin released MacArthur's response, which clashed with the views of the Truman administration on almost every point. The Far East, the general insisted, was more important than Europe and a negotiated settlement in Korea amounted to abject surrender. "If we lose the war to Communism in Asia," the letter warned, "the fall of Europe is inevitable. . . . We must win. There is no substitute for victory." Differing publicly with the administration was serious; interjecting those differences into domestic politics was outrageous, especially since MacArthur had flirted with the Republican Presidential nomination while serving in the Southwest Pacific in 1944. On April 9, after obtaining the concurrence of the Joint Chiefs of Staff, the President directed the Department of the Army to recall MacArthur.

Ridgway replaced MacArthur and Lt. Gen. James A. Van Fleet assumed command of Eighth Army. Both Ridgway and Van Fleet had great confidence in the Eighth Army. Indeed, Van Fleet hoped to execute a landing similar to that at Inchon, this time on the east coast, and repeat the success of September 1950. Ridgway shared the belief that the Chinese in Korea could be defeated, although at a great, perhaps prohibitive cost. The victory, moreover, might well prove meaningless, for Ridgway supported the administration's view that western Europe was the decisive ideological and military battleground in the fight against communism.

General MacArthur returned from the Orient at a time when the Republican leadership, which resented the "loss" of China to communism, was attacking the Democrats for becoming entangled in the North Atlantic Treaty Organization. His appearance seemed a godsend, for here was a popular hero who rejected the idea of Europe first and believed that the Chinese

On a visit to Japan in 1951, the Chief of Staff of the Air Force, General Hoyt S. Vandenberg *(third from right)* inspects an airlift wing with the commander of Far East Air Forces, Lt. Gen. George E. Stratemeyer *(second from left)*; the commander of Fifth Air Force, Maj. Gen. Earle E. Partridge *(fourth from right)*; and the commander of Far East Air Forces Combat Cargo Command, Maj. Gen. William H. Tunner *(second from right)*.

Nationalist armies, although driven from the mainland to a refuge on the island of Taiwan, had received sufficient training and equipment since that debacle to defeat the more numerous Chinese communists. During a hearing before the Armed Services and Foreign Relations Committees of the Senate on the subject of American policy in the Far East, MacArthur demanded that the administration choose among three courses of action: surrender, stalemate, or victory. Surrender was unthinkable. Stalemate, in effect continuing the kind of limited operations begun by Ridgway in February, would kill Chinese, but as time passed American casualties would inevitably mount, making the war progressively less popular and harder to sustain. The only alternative was victory, which could be won by extending the war to mainland China, using Nationalist troops and American air and naval forces.

The Joint Chiefs of Staff rallied behind the President. During the retreat from the Yalu, they had considered a strategy similar to MacArthur's, but only as a last resort if the Chinese overran the Korean peninsula. The Joint Chiefs did not share MacArthur's confidence in the Nationalist forces. The danger of a Chinese triumph had passed, the front had been stabilized, and the Eighth Army had returned to the offensive. As a result, the uniformed leaders of the armed forces were shifting their attention from a secondary theater to the main task of protecting Europe against the Soviet Union, the nation they considered the principal antagonist. The Joint Chiefs were willing to accept a limited war in Korea because they believed that extending the war into China would work to the advantage of the Soviet Union, tying down air, ground, and naval forces needed to support and strengthen the American allies in Europe or to retaliate in case of Soviet aggression. Especially telling was the testimony of General Vandenberg, who combined subtle criticism of MacArthur with a blatant appeal for appropriations when he lamented the fact that his "shoestring air force," though it could devastate the cities of China if directed to do so, would sustain losses that would prevent it from simultaneously deterring or punishing aggression by the Soviet Union.

The members of the two Senate committees, with a majority of Democrats, voted along party lines to vindicate the administration's policy. Despite the acclaim that greeted MacArthur on his return from the Far East, his proposal to expand the conflict aroused little public support. The populace had grown disenchanted with the war in Korea, however much it might admire the general who had directed the advance from Australia to Japan during World War II, served as viceroy over the defeated Japanese, and more recently planned the masterful attack at Inchon. The administration seemed correct in its belief that the best hope was a negotiated settlement; the other side seemed willing to talk, for on June 23, 1951, the Soviet Ambassador to the United Nations publicly called for armistice talks.

Since neither the communist forces nor those of the United Nations could win the war without bloody and dangerous escalation, the idea of negotiations seemed attractive to both sides, but neither would risk negotiating from a position of weakness. Consequently, limited—but often ferocious—battles continued to be fought throughout the process of fashioning a cease-fire. Three months of preliminary discussions at Kaesong in North Korea resulted in the establishment of a small demilitarized zone and the beginning of formal truce negotiations in October 1951 at Panmunjom, a village just south of the 38th parallel. When representatives of the two sides first met at Kaesong, perhaps a million men were serving on the Korean peninsula; when the talks finally ended at Panmunjom, that number had doubled, largely the result of Chinese reinforcements and the formation of new South Korean divisions.

While tens of thousands of these troops battled along the 38th parallel, the cease-fire negotiations proceeded slowly. The principal obstacle to progress was Chinese insistence that all prisoners held by the United Nations be returned to communist control. Many of the captured North Koreans preferred to stay in the South; former Nationalist soldiers impressed into the communist ranks wanted to join their friends and relatives on Taiwan; other Chinese were simply disenchanted with life under communism; and the hard core of Chinese dissidents persuaded or pressured still others into refusing repatriation. The governments of North Korea and China feared a severe blow to their prestige if any sizable number of the 100,000 or more prisoners should refuse to return to a homeland that propagandists celebrated as a paradise for peasants and workers. Both nations therefore insisted that all prisoners be repatriated as a condition of any armistice. This was unacceptable to American authorities, including President Truman, whose collective conscience was haunted by the memory of East Europeans forcibly repatriated to Soviet-occupied territory after World War II.

The ensuing deadlock left some 12,000 prisoners—among them 7,000 South Koreans, 3,000 Americans, and almost 1,000 British—in the hands of the enemy. The treatment they received varied according to the time and circumstances of their capture. The North Korean army, whether advancing arrogantly or in panicky retreat, spared little concern for prisoners, at times taking none or shooting those already in custody. Army Maj. Gen. William F. Dean, himself a prisoner of the North Koreans, recalled that American pilots who parachuted safely after bombing or strafing towns north of the 38th parallel could expect no mercy from any civilians who might capture them. Whereas the treatment afforded by the North Koreans fluctuated between cruelty and neglect, the Chinese saw the prisoners as a valuable propaganda tool, especially the 200 Air Force pilots or air crewmen among them. The Chinese exerted pressure on some of these airmen, and on other prisoners as well, to confess that the United States was practicing germ warfare by dropping insects or infected materials on North Korea. In addition to discrediting the United States, the confessions of germ warfare provided an explanation of recent epidemics of typhus and other diseases that diverted attention from the possibility that the maladies had accompanied the Chinese armies into North Korea. While preventing an international committee of the Red Cross from investigating the charge of germ warfare, the Chinese used torture and starvation to break the resistance of several Air Force prisoners.

The exploitation of captives by the Chinese was investigated by the Department of Defense, which cooperated with Eugene Kinkead, an American journalist, in the writing of *In Every War But One*, a book that in effect blamed the victims as much as it did the captors who abused them. The author argued that only in the Korean War had Americans held prisoner by the enemy collaborated willingly, suffered a breakdown in discipline and morale, and failed to effect a "respectable number" of escapes. He maintained that prisoners of other nationalities had shown greater powers of resistance than the Americans; of the American armed forces, he was most critical of the Army and least so of the Marine Corps. As for the Air Force, he charged that, of the fifty-nine individuals from whom the Chinese had tried to extort confessions of germ warfare, thirty-eight had co-

In June 1951 Secretary of the Air Force Thomas K. Finletter visits the new commander of Far East Air Forces, Lt. Gen. Otto P. Weyland, in Japan. Weyland had just replaced Lt. Gen. George E. Stratemeyer, who was recovering from a heart attack. During the first year of the war, Weyland had been Stratemeyer's Vice Commander for Operations.

operated to some degree, with twenty-three providing usable propaganda. Even as he condemned the overall conduct of the prisoners, he admitted that not enough recognition had been given to those who had resisted. Kinkead's solution, and that of the Department of Defense, was a code of conduct that emphasized resistance and escape, backed by training and indoctrination to achieve these ideals.

Albert Biderman, a sociologist employed for some years by the Air Force, challenged the analysis by Kinkead and the Department of Defense in his book, *March to Calumny*. With the perspective provided by the passage of almost a decade, Biderman compared the behavior of the various nationalities imprisoned by the Chinese and concluded that the Americans did about as well as the others. True, lapses in discipline had occurred and morale had sagged, but much of the so-called collaboration had consisted of cooperating to the least extent possible, such as signing a peace petition or listening to lectures, to avoid mistreatment or possibly death while the truce talks proceeded to their ultimate conclusion. Biderman insisted that the critics had overlooked the fact that many soldiers had been captured in the dead of winter and undergone a demoralizing and debilitating march to the prison camps along the Yalu. Nor had the investigators, in his opinion, understood the ruthlessness of the Chinese in using terror to obtain what proved to be a short-lived harvest of germ warfare propaganda. Given the lack of sympathy for the prisoners among a populace whose towns and villages had been bombed and the inability of the average American to blend in with Korean farmers or laborers, he was surprised that escapes had been attempted and that at least three had succeeded. All in all, Biderman's analysis was less alarming, less of a condemnation, and more accurate than the official view set forth by Kinkead.

Interdiction

While the truce talks dragged on, stymied over the issue of the repatriation of prisoners, air power carried out three general missions: supporting United Nations forces engaged in frontline combat; preparing plans to attack restricted targets in North Korea, such as the hydroelectric plants, in the event that the negotiations collapsed; and preventing the Chinese from massing men and supplies in an attempt to break the stalemate. Essential to all these was maintaining air superiority, the job of the F–86s that patrolled MiG Alley. The missions were being carried out under new leadership, however. General Stratemeyer suffered a heart attack in May 1951 and turned the Far East Air Forces over to Partridge, who served for three weeks until Weyland took over for the remainder of the war. Similarly, Maj. Gen. Edward J. Timberlake, Partridge's vice commander, became interim commander of the Fifth Air Force pending the arrival of Lt. Gen. Frank F. Everest. Command of the Fifth Air Force thereafter became a one-year tour, with Lt. Gens. Glenn O. Barcus and Samuel E. Anderson succeeding to the assignment. Once responsibility for the operation of the combat cargo organization passed in February 1951 from Tunner to Brig. Gen. John F. Henebry, a recently mobilized reservist, that too became a year's tour of duty. Commanders of the Bomber Command were replaced at four-month intervals after Brig. Gen. James E. Briggs took over from General O'Donnell in January 1951.

The standardized tour for most senior commanders reflected an Air Force decision that individuals should serve for a definite period or number of missions to maintain morale, efficiency, and aggressiveness. During 1950, a shortage of pilots and crewmen frustrated this policy, but once personnel became available and the Army adopted a fixed tour in Korea, the Air Force could put such a plan into effect without running short of trained men or undermining morale in another service. The actual length of time that an officer or enlisted man spent in Korea depended upon his assignment and the needs of the Air Force. The Strategic Air Command, for example, usually required a six-month tour but beginning in 1952, an outstanding crew might be rotated a month early, whereas one that was slow to achieve proficiency could be held for a seventh month.

Of the missions conducted under the umbrella of air superiority, interdiction took on special significance in the spring of 1951. As General Ridgway's troops probed toward Seoul and beyond, the enemy's supply lines seemed to present an especially vulnerable target, for they stretched 150 miles or more from the Yalu to the vicinity of the 38th parallel. Designed to take advantage of this apparent vulnerability was Operation Strangle, which shared the name of a similar interdiction campaign conducted in Italy seven years earlier. The choice of this name, which promised so much, represented an effort to stir the enthusiasm of certain senior ground officers who had a jaundiced view of aerial interdiction and doubted that air strikes and armed reconnaissance could achieve the announced goal of paralyzing enemy transportation between the railheads of southern North Korea and the battlefield. In retrospect, a better name might have been Operation Lasso, for air power hobbled the enemy through interdiction without totally destroying his capacity to resist, and to do even that required the combined exertions of both air and ground forces.

In the Korean version of Operation Strangle, the Fifth Air Force, assisted by the Navy's carrier task force and the 1st Marine Aircraft Wing (and to a limited extent by the Bomber Command, Far East Air Forces), tried to deprive the Chinese and North Korean forces of essential supplies. Air Force F–80s and F–84s flew most of the strikes, conducting daylight armed reconnaissance against the roads, bridges, and tunnels that carried truck convoys. The Republic F-84 Thunderjets had arrived in late 1950 with the F–86s. Although inferior to F–86s in air-to-air combat, the F–84s bolstered Fifth Air Force's daylight ground attack capability. Meanwhile B–26s patrolled the highway net during darkness. Strangle began on May 31 and extended through July without having a noticeable effect on the enemy buildup in front of the Eighth Army. Several factors contributed to the disappointing results. The emerging stalemate on the ground, which relieved tactical aircraft of the burden of providing a large volume of close air support, also reduced the enemy's consumption of munitions and other cargo, thus undermining the effectiveness of aerial interdiction by leaving the enemy less dependent on his motorized supply lines. Since the Chinese and North Koreans neither mounted nor were forced to repel large-scale attacks, they could adjust their supply effort to take advantage of the main weakness of Operation Strangle—an inability to conduct sustained attacks by night or in bad weather. Traffic moved with near impunity through darkness or rain, for aircrews had to rely on flares or moonlight to locate targets. Damaged roads and bridges were quickly repaired or bypassed, and the damage inflicted from the sky was not as severe as hoped because intense antiaircraft fire reduced bombing accuracy in daylight. Nevertheless, interdiction continued, al-

This North Korean railyard at Hwangju, had, by December 1951, been repeatedly bombed.

though against a broader range of targets, at times accompanied by great fanfare and arousing unrealistic expectations.

Except for occasional attacks on bridges or segments of highway in connection with Operation Strangle, the B–29s normally contributed to interdiction by conducting daylight raids on rail lines, marshaling yards, or warehouses. After October 1951, when MiGs slipped past patrolling F–86s and downed five B–29s in a single week, the bomber command began attacking exclusively at night. The change of tactics enhanced the safety of men and aircraft but decreased bombing accuracy. Fortunately, because of the recurring bad weather in Korea, the command had already set up a short-range navigation system, the shoran network of radio beacons on the ground. This aid to aerial navigation enabled the bombers to locate and attack such area targets as large villages, rail complexes, or warehouse districts. In response to shoran-guided night raids, the enemy employed radar-controlled searchlights in conjunction with antiaircraft batteries. Electronic warfare ensued, during which B–29s, the underside of the wings and fuselage camouflaged with black paint, relied on chaff and jamming transmitters to frustrate radar operators on the ground.

When the change from day to night tactics occurred, the B–29s were in the midst of another systematic interdiction effort. This campaign, for a time also called Operation Strangle, began in August 1951 and was directed against the rail net. Enthusiastic advocates on the staff of Fifth Air Force believed that air attacks could constrict the volume of rail traffic, forcing the enemy to rely on trucks, which were in short supply and carried less cargo than freight cars. Some of these officers went so far as to predict that Chinese and North Korean troops, deprived of essential food and ammunition, would have to retreat to shorten vulnerable lines of supply. F–84s joined F–80s in attacking various rail choke points and B–29s bombed bridges; but the big bombers had to attack at night using shoran. As had happened in the earlier Operation Strangle, antiaircraft fire affected the accuracy of fighter-bombers, and work crews moved swiftly to repair damage or build bypasses.

Although the second Operation Strangle did not achieve its most optimistic goal of forcing the enemy to retreat, the attacks prevented the accumulation of enough supplies to mount a major offensive. As a result, rail interdiction continued into 1952 but without the ill-starred title of Strangle. An intensified and redesignated program of rail interdiction, Operation , began on February 25 and became a race between American airmen trying to obliterate the rail lines and Korean laborers trying to repair them. On a single mission, as many as forty B–29s hit a bridge, a mission that formerly might have been assigned to eight of the bombers; and fighter-bombers lavished 500 or more bombs on a single length of track. This kind of work from both Air Force and Marine squadrons, impressive though it was in terms of effort, could maintain no more than six cuts on North Korea's main rail lines, too few to do more than inconvenience the enemy.

During SATURATE, intelligence analysts found one segment of rail line that seemed especially vulnerable to B–29s using shoran. The target was a railroad overpass at Wadong on the main east-west supply route. Here, deep in a gorge, the railway crossed a highway, so that bombs missing the railroad viaduct might detonate against the rock wall of the defile, causing landslides that would block both the tracks and the road. Unfortunately the bridge proved hard to hit and the rock sides of the gorge were all but impervious to the effects of 500-pound bombs. After six weeks of effort, from January 26 through March 11, 1952, 1,000 tons of high explosives had produced no landslides, and only one percent of the bombs hit either the viaduct or the highway it crossed. American intelligence estimated that during the attacks the road had been blocked for just seven days and the rail line for four.

What was needed to improve the effectiveness of interdiction was not more bombs dropped from high-flying B–29s but a low-altitude aircraft that could locate and destroy truck convoys and trains moving at night. As early as the first Korean version of Operation Strangle in the spring of 1951, Air Force B–26s and Marine Corps night fighters had patrolled assigned roads or rail lines and attacked traffic by the light of flares. To help the B–26s carry out nighttime armed reconnaissance, Fifth Air Force tried to adapt a Navy-developed searchlight used during World War II by airships searching for submarines. Capt. John S. Walmsley was shot down as he used the light to illuminate a train for another B–26; his heroism in the face of antiaircraft fire resulted in the posthumous award of the Medal of Honor. Because the light attracted fire from the ground, B–26 crews came to rely on flares for night attack. Claims of trucks destroyed mounted into the thousands, but verification of the damage inflicted at night proved so difficult that no evaluation of the effectiveness of nighttime interdiction was possible.

The difficulty of conducting demonstrably effective aerial interdiction gave ammunition to those critics who wanted the Air Force to use more of its aircraft for close air support and use them more effectively. The Fifth Air Force in Korea had come to emphasize interdiction because the enemy seemed more vulnerable to attack along his exposed lines of supply and communications than in his bunkers on the battlefield. In contrast, Army commanders wanted air strikes to supplement mortars and artillery in the battles that flared suddenly and subsided throughout the period of stalemate. A solution proposed by Army officers serving in Korea was to have a Marine Corps fighter squadron assigned to each of the three Army corps in Korea. General Weyland succeeded in blocking this end run past the joint operations center, but he did change the allocations of sorties between interdiction and close air support. During the two Strangle operations, the Fifth Air Force flew ten times as many interdiction as close support sorties, which declined to fewer than 500 a month. After the spring of 1952, Air

Force close air support sorties averaged about 2,000 per month, or nearly half the number of interdiction sorties.

Moreover, an improved command and control network enabled the Fifth Air Force to respond more quickly to calls for emergency support than it had in the early months of the war. A request from a tactical air control party assigned to a regiment could pass through division and corps headquarters and reach the joint operations center at Seoul in as little as 10 minutes. From the joint operations center, which approved or rejected the requests, instructions went next door to the tactical air control center, in effect the communications link that forwarded orders to the appropriate wing headquarters or to aircraft already aloft. The responding pilot first checked in with one of the recently established tactical air direction posts, which were assigned to each American corps and equipped with radar for handling night strikes. In daylight the pilot then proceeded to the forward air controller selected by the joint operations center, reporting for instructions to a fellow aviator who might be flying in a T–6 or on the ground with a tactical air control party. The total time between initial request and the resulting fighter strike was around 40 minutes, possibly less, depending upon whether the aircraft was diverted from another mission or launched from an airfield where it had been standing alert. At night, instead of assigning the strike to a controller on or above the battlefield, the joint operations center usually relied on a tactical air direction post located about 10 miles behind the lines. This control agency used radar to guide the attacking aircraft, usually B–26s or B–29s with radar transponders for easier tracking, against some predetermined target, perhaps troops advancing through some previously plotted area or a suspected Chinese command post. Close support of ground forces remained an important mission throughout the war, one that was carried out by dedicated airmen, none more so than Maj. Charles Loring. On November 22, 1952, he flew his crippled F–80 into a gun emplacement that was firing on American troops. Major Loring was posthumously awarded the Medal of Honor, and Loring Air Force Base, Maine, was named in his honor.

Air Pressure

Beginning during the summer of 1952, after a year of stalemate, the air war over Korea entered a new phase, an attempt to employ air power to pressure the Chinese into accepting an armistice satisfactory to the United States. The arrival of a new United Nations commander, Gen. Mark W. Clark, who replaced Ridgway in May 1952, signaled an expansion of the air effort, for Clark believed that the deadlock at Panmunjom had to be broken and that "air pressure" afforded the least costly means of doing so. As a result, Clark accepted Weyland's recommendation to attack the hydroelectric plants in North Korea, cutting off power throughout the country and impressing on the leadership the consequences of delaying a settlement. The Fifth Air Force and Task Force 77, with Weyland as coordinating agent, drew up plans for such a campaign. So impressed were the members of the Joint Chiefs of Staff that they persuaded President Truman to include the Sui-ho power plant on the Yalu River in the list of targets. With a general election to take place in November, the President, too, was eager to achieve a ceasefire. Air Force and Navy fighter-bombers attacked 17 hydroelectric generating plants in four separate complexes—Sui-ho, Chosin, Fusen, and Kyosen—during the last week of June 1952. After more than 1,200 sorties, 11 of the generating facilities lay in ruins; North Korea experienced a nearly total loss of electric power lasting two weeks and did not achieve its former level of generating capacity before the end of the war, some 13 months later. The destruction of the Sui-ho power plant, one of the largest hydroelectric facilities in the world, also reduced Manchuria's supply of electricity by nearly a fourth. During the attacks, antiaircraft fire succeeded in downing only two aircraft, both flown by naval aviators who were rescued, and there were no losses to MiGs. Indeed, on the first day of the raids, most of the 250 MiGs based at An-tung, within 40 miles of Sui-ho, fled farther into Manchuria as though under the impression that their airfields might be the target. Although tactically successful, the disruption of the power grid did not bring progress in the talks at Panmunjom.

When the bombing of the hydroelectric plants failed to break the deadlock in the truce negotiations, the United Nations Command launched air attacks against other targets. During the summer of 1952, Air Force and Navy aircraft carried out the two biggest raids of the war, both against Pyongyang, North Korea's capital. These were the first major attacks on the city since January 1951, shortly after Chinese forces had captured it, when more than a hundred B–29s dropped incendiary clusters in an unsuccessful raid. The failure of the January attack to destroy more than a third of the city was attributed to snow, which retarded the spread of the flames, and an excessively tight bombing pattern. When attacking in 1952, Air Force bombers did not drop incendiary clusters, judged less accurate than high explosives and more likely to cause widespread collateral damage. The Truman administration wanted accuracy against Pyongyang, mainly to protect American prisoners of war believed held there. Other towns harboring large concentrations of enemy troops or stocks of supplies were attacked with incendiary clusters or napalm, along with high explosives.

On July 11, 1952, United Nations fighter-bombers flew 1,200 sorties and B–29s flew 54 against the North Korean capital. Radio Pyongyang attributed 7,000 casualties and the destruction of 1,500 buildings to this raid, and reports from intelligence agents indicated that a direct hit had destroyed the headquarters of the North Korean Ministry of Industry. Despite the effects of this attack, Generals Weyland and Clark decided to send 1,400 sorties by Air Force and Navy fighter-bombers against surviving warehouses, barracks, and public buildings in Pyongyang. Delivered on August 29, this additional blow satisfied a request by the Department of State for some dramatic military action during a visit to the Soviet Union by China's premier, Chou En-lai (Zhou Enlai). The American ambassador at Moscow, George Kennan, suggested that if the Chinese could be pressured into increasing their demands for aid from the Soviet Union, the Soviet leadership might decide that the nation's resources would be strained and urge China to accept a truce. Unfortunately, the August raid on Pyongyang was no more successful than the July attack in prodding the Chinese toward a truce.

The conflict in Korea had dragged on for more than twenty-seven months and had become a political issue by November 1952, when the United States held a Presidential election. The Republican candidate, Gen. Dwight D. Eisenhower, the supreme Allied commander in Europe during World War II, faced a Democrat, Governor Adlai E. Stevenson of Illinois, who lacked military experience. Eisenhower called for greater South Korean participation in the fighting and promised that if elected he would go to Korea, presumably to find a solution to the impasse there. He was elected, went to Korea late in November without waiting to take the oath of office, and returned determined to break the stalemate in the talks at Panmunjom. The likeliest means of doing so was through military pressure, but conventional air and ground operations had failed to force China and North Korea to agree to an acceptable cease-fire. Consequently his thoughts turned first to Nationalist China and then to the atomic bomb.

Immediately after taking office in January 1953, President Eisenhower announced that the United States Navy would no longer patrol the waters separating the Nationalists on Taiwan from the Chinese mainland. Since the outbreak of war in Korea, American warships had in effect neutralized Taiwan,

During four days in late June 1952, the Air Force and the Navy cooperated to destroy eleven hydroelectric power plants and plunge North Korea into a power blackout for two weeks. For the rest of the war, North Korea was left with a fraction of its former power production capacity .

preventing Chiang Kai-shek (Jiang Jieshi) from trying to realize his dream, however unrealistic, of invading the continent. Now Chiang was unleashed, and those who joked about his prospects of reconquering China missed the purpose of this action. By means of this essentially symbolic gesture, Eisenhower was showing his willingness to widen the war if an armistice did not soon emerge.

Regarding the possibility of using atomic weapons in a wider war, the new President moved more slowly. He consulted the Joint Chiefs of Staff, who initially offered conflicting advice: Vandenberg suggested that atomic bombs, if used, be directed against Manchuria as well as North Korea; Bradley warned that a renewed ground offensive without atomic firepower would produce a staggering toll of American casualties; and Gen. J. Lawton Collins, now the Army Chief of Staff, said that recent tests in the Nevada desert indicated that Chinese troops deeply entrenched along a 150-mile front would provide a poor target for tactical nuclear weapons. The administration considered a variety of options for increasing the pressure on China, but by the end of May 1953 it had become obvious that any intensification of military pressure would extend the war to China and that an attack on China would require the use of atomic weapons.

Although willing to expand the conflict and use atomic bombs if that became necessary, the President and his advisers tried first to exert a more subtle form of pressure that might make it unnecessary to broaden the fighting. President Eisenhower and his Secretary of State, John Foster Dulles, saw to it that word reached the Chinese government of America's willingness to resort to nuclear weapons to break the impasse, hoping that the threat alone would persuade China to accept a suitable armistice.

As the Eisenhower administration was shaping this policy, other events affected the future of the two Koreas. On March 4, 1953, Stalin died, ending three decades during which the Soviet Union conformed to the dictates of this one man. Georgi Malenkov, nominally the successor of Stalin, lacked the power to rule without the consent of certain of his colleagues, notably Lavrenti F. Beria, the head of the secret police. The struggle for control of the Soviet Union took precedence over the conduct of an aggressive foreign policy, and Malenkov called for an easing of tensions with the West. Indeed, he may have pressured China and North Korea to end the war. By the end of March, China displayed its willingness to compromise by agreeing to an exchange of sick and wounded prisoners of war. Because of the humanitarian character of the action and the small number involved—7,300 men, 90 percent Chinese and North Korean, the rest soldiers of the United Nations Command, including just 149 Americans—the issue of forced repatriation did not surface.

While the President and his advisers discussed the possible use of the atomic bomb, the conventional air war against North Korea continued, as B–29s and Fifth Air Force fighter-bombers attacked a new target—the nation's irrigation dams. General Clark, in looking for new ways to pressure the enemy, discovered twenty of these structures, none of which had yet been attacked. Early in 1953, the Far East Air Forces concluded that breaching all of the dams would utterly destroy an entire year's rice crop. Both Clark and Weyland viewed such a campaign as the ultimate form of aerial pressure, and when the truce talks again stalled, they decided to go ahead. During May 1953 air attacks shattered three dams, releasing impounded water that not only swept away rice plants but also flooded roads, rail lines, and even an airfield. Indeed, General Clark insisted that the destruction of just the first of the three dams to be attacked "was as effective as weeks of railroad interdiction." Yet, as was true with damaged rail lines, laborers quickly repaired the breaks, and the North Koreans lowered the level of water behind the dams so a rupture would not release a wall of water like that which caused so much damage in the first three attacks. However, reducing the volume of water behind the structures also reduced the water available to irrigate the rice crop that fed the people of North Korea.

Aware of the threat of atomic war, unsure of the new leadership in Moscow, and bled by sustained fighting, the Chinese in early June 1953 seemed ready to sign an armistice satisfactory to the United States. But what Americans found suitable did not please South Korean President Rhee, who balked at accepting a permanently divided Korea. To demonstrate his displeasure, he permitted some 25,000 North Koreans in United Nations prisoner of war camps to "escape," actually drafting a sizable number into the South Korean army. Perhaps to punish

Rhee for his intransigence or merely to gain the initiative before the fighting ended, the enemy launched the most savage offensive since the first year of the war. In response, Air Force close air support sorties increased by 40 percent to almost 7,500 during June, and MiGs appeared over North Korea in greater numbers than before, but suffered their greatest losses—F–86 pilots claimed more than 100, including 16 on June 30 alone. Meanwhile, fighter-bombers and B–29s continued to batter North Korean airfields. Earlier, airfields had been hit to prevent the Chinese from deploying the short-range MiGs close to the battlefield; now the purpose of the attacks was to prevent the communists from increasing aerial strength in the weeks before the signing of an armistice that would forbid the shipment of additional military equipment into Korea. The Chinese succeeded, however, in hiding an estimated 200 aircraft in the countryside near Sinuiju.

Representatives of China, North Korea, and the United States signed an armistice on July 27, 1953. South Korea refused to sign, but threats to cut off American aid apparently persuaded the Rhee government to honor the truce. As expected, the prisoner exchange proved embarrassing to the communists, who had at last abandoned their demand for forced repatriation. Of more than 20,000 Chinese prisoners in the hands of the United Nations, two-thirds rejected repatriation, whereas only 21 of the 3,000 Americans in enemy hands chose to remain behind, along with 327 South Koreans and one British serviceman.

There may be no single, unambiguous reason why the Chinese and North Koreans finally relented on the prisoner issue and ended the war. President Eisenhower believed in retrospect that his threat to wage atomic war against China was decisive. Other factors contributing to a settlement may have included the death of Stalin and the uncertainty that followed as his possible successors grappled for power. Yet, had Stalin lived and Eisenhower not threatened to use the atomic bomb, the cumulative cost of the fighting might nevertheless have forced China to yield. The United Nations Command, which lost some 450,000 killed or wounded, estimated that Chinese and North Korean military casualties were at least three times greater. Of the four major participants, America's losses of 35,000 killed and 100,000 wounded were by far the least. The South Korean

Pilot ejects from downed MiG. The victor in this combat was Edwin E. Aldrin, later one of the first astronauts to walk on the moon.

armed forces suffered some 300,000 casualties, but despite this toll of dead or wounded, most of South Korea had been sheltered since mid-1951 from the desolation of war. As a result of that period of freedom from enemy occupation, along with the training and military assistance provided by the United States, when the fighting ended South Korea's army was twice as large as North Korea's and was growing faster.

The air war had been very destructive. Far East Air Forces estimated that it had killed nearly 150,000 North Korean and Chinese troops and destroyed more than 950 aircraft, 800 bridges, 1,100 tanks, 800 locomotives, 9,000 railroad cars,

70,000 motor vehicles, and 80,000 buildings. This damage was inflicted at the cost of 1,200 airmen killed and 750 aircraft destroyed by the enemy. For the first time, air supremacy and the helicopter permitted the frequent rescue of aviators shot down behind enemy lines, thus reducing the death toll. The Air Rescue Service retrieved 170 Air Force pilots or crewmen from enemy territory, more than 10 percent of those who went down there.

As General Bradley pointed out during Senate hearings into American policy in the Far East, the existence of sanctuaries benefited both sides. Chinese air bases in Manchuria were not attacked, but Chinese aircraft did not bomb or strafe the front-line positions of the United Nations forces and made no effort to disrupt the enormous volume of cargo moving through South Korean ports to the battlefield. Had the United States attacked Manchuria, however, the Soviet Union might have given the Chinese long-range bombers capable of striking targets in South Korea or even Japan from bases north of the Yalu. Similarly, neither side attacked the other's ocean-going shipping, although the Americans did wage war on the North Korean fishing fleet. No communist power challenged the passage of the ships and aircraft that carried a million tons of American military supplies across the Pacific each month, depositing their cargo in huge depots in Japan, which themselves would have been vulnerable to air attack. American forces had worked a logistical miracle in supplying the United Nations Command, but they did so without air and naval opposition.

American airmen dropped more than 500,000 tons of bombs during the war, all directed against targets in Korea. Far East Air Forces, including Fifth Air Force, contributed two-thirds, an amount that exceeded the weight of the conventional bombardment of Japan in World War II. Yet, the weight of bombs expended in Korea was less significant than the weapon not used, for the first country to acquire nuclear weapons and use them in combat had this time withheld them and engaged in a limited, conventional war.

The outbreak of fighting in Korea and the nature of the conflict there caused the Air Force to separate the Tactical Air Command from the Continental Air Command. Although the Air Force made this concession to the needs of limited, conventional warfare, it did not develop aircraft specifically for tactical operations. In spite of the need for a higher performance aircraft to replace the T–6 and operate from crude airstrips, none was forthcoming, nor was an attempt made to develop special types for close air support or night interdiction. The ideal tactical fighter was envisioned officially as a multipurpose aircraft capable of strafing, dropping bombs, and engaging enemy fighters. Even the F–86, which had proved so deadly against the MiG in aerial combat, appeared in a fighter-bomber version that saw combat late in the war. The emphasis on versatility ran counter to the beliefs of Colonel Gabreski and like-minded veterans of MiG Alley who were convinced that the air battles of the future would be won by a fast day-fighter, stripped of all nonessential equipment, easy to fly, and simple to maintain. Clarence L. "Kelly" Johnson, an engineer for Lockheed aircraft, designed the F–104 to be just such an airplane; but it rapidly gained weight, increased in complexity, and by the time production ended appeared as a fighter-bomber.

In many ways the Korean conflict proved frustrating for the Air Force. A combination of terrain and camouflage thwarted aerial surveillance during the Chinese buildup south of the Yalu River in October and November 1950. A fleet of aging B–29s destroyed almost every vestige of industry in North Korea, but armaments from nations whose factories could not be bombed satisfied North Korea's needs. Absolute control of the air did not ensure victory on the ground, for the enemy's transportation system survived sustained air attacks and provided the volume of supplies necessary for an essentially static war, marked after the spring of 1951 by only limited offensives. The emphasis should be placed, however, on the accomplishments of air power: supplying the ground forces; eliminating the threat of aerial attack on the movement and logistical support of the United Nations Command; and, in general, serving as a means, less costly in American lives than a succession of even limited offensives, of maintaining pressure on the enemy in a war that rapidly became unpopular in the United States. Perhaps the conventional bombing of North Korea gave the Chinese and Soviet leadership a hint of the destruction that would result from the atomic warfare that President Eisenhower was threatening.

The Air Force had entered the war committed to the heavy bomber armed with atomic weapons; to a strategy of deterrence; and, should deterrence fail, to a retaliatory strike designed, insofar as aircraft and numbers of weapons permitted, to destroy the enemy's capacity for war. Far from undermining these principles, three years of limited warfare had reinforced them, persuading the leadership of the Air Force that the United States should stand ready to attack the Soviet Union and not divert its strength against aggression by proxy. As a result, during the Senate hearing that followed the relief of MacArthur, when Vandenberg complained about his shoestring Air Force, bemoaning its inability to wage atomic war against both the Soviet Union and China, he was more concerned about worldwide deterrence or retaliation than tactical operations in Korea. Moreover, in his opinion the North Korean invasion of the South did not mean that deterrence had failed—after all, the Soviet Union had not taken advantage of the war in the Far East by attacking elsewhere—but suggested that the deterrent force should be made stronger. He saw the Soviet Union as the main enemy in any future war, and the industrial base that supported it could be destroyed only by using nuclear weapons. The threat of total devastation seemed the likeliest means to prevent aggression by the Soviet Union and its satellite states, or so it appeared in 1953.

Suggested Readings

Chen Jian. *China's Road to the Korean War.* New York: Columbia University Press, 1994.

Cooling, Benjamin Franklin, ed. *Case Studies in the Achievement of Air Superiority.* Washington: Center for Air Force History, 1994.

Cooling, Benjamin Franklin, ed. *Case Studies in the Development of Close Air Support.* Washington: Center for Air Force History, 1990.

Cumings, Bruce. *The Origins of the Korean War.* 2 vols. Princeton: Princeton University Press, 198–90.

Fehrenbach, T. R. *This Kind of War.* New York: Macmillan, 1963.

Futrell, Robert Frank. *The United States Air Force in Korea, 1950–1953.* Washington: Center for Air Force History, 1991 (reprint).

Goncharov, Sergei N., John W. Lewis and Xue Litai. *Uncertain Partners: Stalin, Mao, and the Korean War.* Stanford: Stanford University Press, 1993.

Goulden, Joseph C. *Korea: The Untold Story of the War.* New York: Times Books, 1982.

Hallion, Richard P. *The Naval Air War in Korea.* Annapolis: Nautical & Aviation, 1986.

Leffler, Melvyn P. *A Preponderance of Power: National Security, the Truman Administration and the Cold War.* Stanford: Stanford University Press, 1992.

Mark, Eduard. *Aerial Interdiction in Three Wars.* Washington: Center for Air Force History, 1994.

Moody, Walton S. *Building A Strategic Air Force.* Washington: Air Force History and Museums Program, 1996.

Pape, Robert A. *Bombing to Win: Air Power and Coercion in War.* Ithaca: Cornell University Press, 1996.

Stueck, William. *The Korean War: An International History.* Princeton: Princeton University Press, 1995.

Williams, William J. *A Revolutionary War: Korea and the Transformation of the Postwar World.* Chicago: Imprint Publications, 1992.

Winnefeld, James A. and Dana J. Johnson. *Joint Air Operations: Pursuit of Unity in Command and Control, 1942–1991.* Annapolis: Naval Institute, 1993.

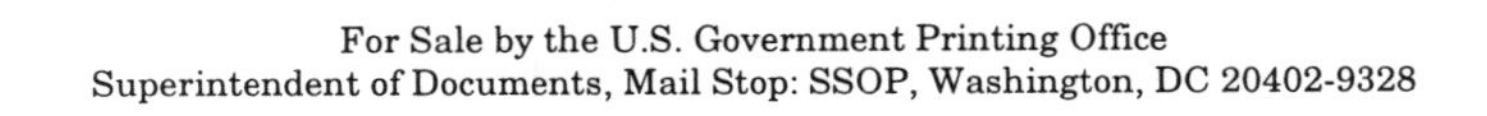
For Sale by the U.S. Government Printing Office
Superintendent of Documents, Mail Stop: SSOP, Washington, DC 20402-9328